SOVEREIGN THOUGHT

The Philosopher & the Kingdom

From Ancient Greece to the *Arthaśāstra*

GWENDOLYN TAUNTON

978-0-6456700-0-4

Sovereign Thought:
The Philosopher and the Kingdom

Gwendolyn Taunton

Thema Classification: QD (Philosophy), QDX (Popular Philosophy), 1QBAG (Ancient Greece), QHDC (Indian Philosophy).

MANTICORE PRESS
WWW.MANTICORE.PRESS

Lives of great men all remind us
We can make our lives sublime,
And departing, leave behind us
Footprints on the sands of time.

– Henry Wadsworth Longfellow,
A Psalm of Life

CONTENTS

PART I

PHILOSOPHY & THE STATE

The Aristocratic Principle in Ancient Greece

I. Introduction 13
II. Origins 15
III. The Polis 23
IV. Demokratia 33
V. Socrates 39
VI. Areté 57
VII. Plato 65
VIII. The State 75
IX. Conclusion 81

PART II

VEDIC TRADITION
&
THE ARTHAŚĀSTRA

The Principle of Sovereignty in India

I. Introduction	95
II. Varuṇa	99
III. Sovereignty & Tradition	107
IV. Cāṇakya & the Mauryan Empire	125
V. The Cakravartin	133
VI. The Arthaśāstra	147
VII. Conclusion	155

PART I

PHILOSOPHY
&
THE STATE

The Aristocratic Principle in Ancient Greece

For I am certain, O men of Athens, that if I had engaged in politics, I should have perished long ago, and done no good either to you or to myself. And don't be offended at my telling you the truth: for the truth is, that no man who goes to war with you or any other multitude, honestly struggling against the commission of unrighteousness and wrong in the State, will save his life; he who will really fight for the right, if he would live even for a little while, must have a private station and not a public one.

– Plato, *The Trial and Death of Socrates*[1]

---

1 *The Republic and Other Works by Plato*, trans. Benjamin Jowett (New York: Doubleday, 1960), 473.

I. INTRODUCTION

ARISTOCRACY AROSE DEEP in the archaic period of ancient Greek history, stemming from an epoch where history predates the written word. Early Hellenic political thought can only be traced back via oral traditions, such as the works of Homer. From these scant references, we are granted an exclusive view of the ancient past via the lens of history. The development and growth of aristocracy in Greece begins here, with its power structure becoming formalized later via the expansion of the *polis*. The advent of democracy is also documented, with the most infamous instance of a clash betwixt the old aristocracy and the new democratic government cited by Plato to be found in his account of the trial of Socrates, who was sentenced to death on charges of impiety and corrupting the youth. Socrates' execution was a great scandal for this era, and it deeply affected Plato. He continued the work of Socrates throughout his entire life, creating some of the most famous works of European philosophy. Similar ideas were also advocated by another famous philosopher, Aristotle, and eventually reached their final culmination in the form of Alexander the

Great. Thus, by an ideological process of learning and education, the aristocracy was restored in one of the world's most formidable empires – that of the God-King, Alexander of Macedon.

Democracy did not endure in Greece for a straightforward reason: It was not an "organic" system of the State.[2] Monarchy was the first form of government in Greece, and democracy was developed only as a replacement. It was therefore not a naturally arising form of social legislation, but rather one created for a particular task. The condition which brought democracy to power was not its essential benefit as a political philosophy, but rather the flaws inherent in the aristocratic system it was created to replace. Aristocracy in Greece essentially castrated itself via internal corruption and decadence.

For the sake of clarity, however, neither Hellenic aristocracy nor democracy are comparable to the way such terms are used today.

---

2 The use of the term "organic" to describe the State will be explained later in this book.

II. ORIGINS

THE ORIGINS OF aristocracy in Greece are older than recorded history, dating back to the composition of the *Iliad* and the *Odyssey* as orally transmitted epics. From them it is possible to glimpse the aristocratic principle in its earliest formative period. The notion of aristocracy arose in Greece simultaneously with civilization, which was itself born during this era. The characteristics found in the heroes of these epics are the same qualities that ancient Greek society deemed to be desirable, such as personal honor and individual strength. These traits were then transcribed into a moral and ethical system that operated as the standard for leadership. Those select few individuals who embodied these qualities quickly elevated their status in that era and came to occupy positions of authority.

This period of history was one of development in Greece, and minimal levels of social order and stratification were in place. Legislation and organization were very much at a rudimentary level. It was nevertheless a formative stage where the social doctrine was primarily built from the ground up, laying the foundations for the future civilization of Hellas[3] to be born. The leaders who rose to power in this epoch did so by their merit, and were the ancestors of the Greek aristocrats. These first few rulers then passed on their power to the next generation, expecting that their traits would be inherited via the royal bloodline. Even today, the famous term "blueblood" is associated with the possession of aristocratic ancestry. Aristocrats then married other aristocrats; the bloodline of the kings was firmly cemented, and power passed only into the hands of those who could claim status by descent. But what were these character traits which could bequeath sacred authority to mortal men?

The answer lies in the structure of the Homeric epics themselves, which depict the society of archaic Greece as a heroic warrior culture. Greece's first leaders came to be so because they were skilled in war and combat – not in a brutish sense, but in a heroic one that required social and strategic skills as well as mere physical force. The desirable qualities in this first phase of Greek aristocracy were closely aligned with the Homeric Ideal. This Ideal required standards of ethics and personal behavior, which is illustrated in the epics by the use of terms such as good (*agathos*, *esthlos*) and bad (*kakos*); these refer almost exclusively to the sphere of physical excellence and bravery, with *agathos* in particular, being conferred upon high-status warriors.[4] The concept of *areté* (excellence) is also of extreme importance in understanding the Hellenic aristocracy's nature. Tyrtaeus here provides

[3] Hellas is the original name for Greece.

[4] Walter Donlan, *The Aristocratic Ideal and Selected Papers* (Wauconda, Ill.: Bolchazy-Carducci Publishers, Inc., 1999), 32.

the following description of *areté* for the Homeric warrior here:

> For a man is not *agathos* in war, unless he endure seeing the bloody slaughter, and stand close reach out for the foe. This is *areté*, this is the best and loveliest prize for the young man to win. A common good this, for the whole *polis* and all the *demos*, when a man holds, firm-set among the fighters, unflinchingly.[5]

Areté is a highly ambiguous word encompassing both *excellence* and *honor* (*timé*): honor. *Timé* was an essential quality for the warrior ethos in this period, but it began to wane when the tribal kingdoms grew in size to form the *polis*. These two concepts are the key to understanding the aristocratic principle, with *areté* in particular functioning as the Hellenic aristocracy's vital core. In this early period, *areté* could be conferred due to individual merit and value to society. The first kings were chosen because they were the best of men; their heirs were selected out of a belief that these good qualities were inherited via the bloodline. Because of the twin requirements of *areté* and *timé*, winning respect from peers was a mandatory task for aspiring leaders; it was therefore a "shame culture" rather than a "guilt culture."[6] This is the fundamental difference between Hellenic and Hebraic cultures, which are usually indexed in terms

---

5 Ibid., 41.

6 Gemino Abad, "Iliad and Odyssey: Areté and Timé" in *The Passion of Virtue: Pathos and Arête in Western Literature* (Singapore: Singapore Management University, 2003), 2-3.

of *shame culture* and *guilt culture*, respectively.[7] Evidence of shame being used as a social mechanism is witnessed here when Paris fails to adhere to the warrior ethos:

> Then Hector rebuked his brother (Paris) with shaming words: "You miserable disgrace, most handsome of men but woman-crazed, a seducer, a selfish fool, I wish you had never been born or had died unmarried – a cause of contempt like this, whom good men despise. The Achaeans must now be mocking us, laughing out loud and saying, 'Some champion they have! Just a pretty face, a man without any strength, without any courage.'"[8]

This is still not the type of aristocracy most people are familiar with, but rather an earlier proto-aristocratic manifestation. When speaking of the Homeric aristocracy, Starr says that "the Homeric world had not yet traveled all the way toward the elaboration of an aristocratic ethos, i.e., an obligatory pattern of life and values consciously conceived and shared by a limited group which considered itself 'best' and the claims of which were generally accepted, even cherished, by other elements of society."[9] It had therefore not yet become what is recognizable today as aristocracy. In this phase, *areté*, and consequently aristocracy, were bestowed on those who had achieved excellence through individual merit and

7 Ibid., 7.

8 Homer, trans. Stephen Mitchell, *The Iliad: A New Translation* (London: Orion Books, 2011), 44.

9 Donlan, *The Aristocratic Ideal*, 25.

martial prowess. This was not always based on physical strength, however, as can be seen when Odysseus rebukes Achilles. He says that "you are stronger than I am and greater by not a little with the spear, yet I, in turn, might overpass you in wisdom (*noēma*) by far."[10] In terms of *areté* and *timé*, the contrast between Achilles and Odysseus is clear:

> In the *Iliad*, the hero stands against other heroes; in the *Odyssey*, the individual stands against the group as a homogeneous mass or collectively: Odysseus against mutinous sailors; Odysseus and Telemachus and Penelope against more than a hundred Suitors. Achilles is heroic, Odysseus more like other men: he has human attachments – food, family, material comfort – while Achilles seems detached from such things.[11]

Achilles' achievement is individual; Odysseus' accomplishment is over other men. Here *areté* is presented in a nebulous manner, suggesting that its social importance had yet to be officially defined. Value was recognized, but it was not explicitly labeled or explained. In this early period of Homeric aristocracy, *areté* simply meant "excellence of any kind; a fast runner displays the *areté* of his feet, and a son excels his father in every kind of *areté* – as athlete, as soldier, and in mind."[12] It was conceived

---

10 Ibid., 19.

11 Abad, " Iliad and Odyssey," 5.

12 Tim Burns, *Organisation and Social Order* (unfinished and unpublished work, 1997, available at web.archive.org/web/20170206094818/http://www.sociology.ed.ac.uk/tomburns/manuscript.html), 18.

of as a personal glory and a state of honor which increased one's social standing and fame, as we see here:

> And someone will say, in a generation far distant, as he sails in his swift ship over the wine-dark sea: "This is the funeral mound of some great man who in ancient times was killed by glorious Hector." Thus he will speak, and my honor will never die.[13]

Homeric Greece was a "shame" culture, but it was also one of glorification; the acquisition of glory and honor were regarded as a tremendous personal achievement. *Philotimia*, or love of honor, was connected with *areté* as well as *timé* since both are qualities found in heroes. In the quest for excellence and honor there were dangers, however. As Aristotle points out, one must avoid *hamartia*, an error or flaw that causes misfortune, which is capable of bringing even heroes to their knees. *Hybris*,[14] meaning arrogance or excessive pride, is one of the best examples of *hamartia*, which can befall the aspiring hero. It is a standard plot device in ancient Greek narratives. One example of this occurs when Achilles, believing himself to be invulnerable, displays aspects of *hybris* by insulting Agamemnon:

> Drunkard, dog-face, quivering deer-hearted coward, you have never dared to arm with your soldiers for battle or go on a raid where only the bravest survive – oh no, you avoid that

---

13 Homer, *The Iliad*, 112.

14 Alternative spelling of *hubris*.

> like death; you would much rather stay safe, right here in the camp and direct your efforts to stealing the prize of whoever might contradict you.[15]

Hybris appears to have been a strong temptation for the Moirai,[16] who operated similarly to *karma* in Greek literature. For those who did possess significant *areté*, *hybris* was a real and present danger. The goal of the Homeric hero was to attain social prominence via *areté*, which was largely dependent on martial prowess. Success in combat provided the mechanism to achieve social recognition in this era, which was devoid of a rigid social structure. With this came other rewards. As these warriors conquered more land, they also accumulated wealth as well as power. The next developmental stage for the aristocracy was therefore for wealth to become a physical indication of success. Material prosperity implied that they were successful; how else could they have acquired it if they were not in some way superior? To a skeptical audience, wealth offered indisputable physical evidence.

But the wealth of the Homeric aristocracy was hard-won in battle, unlike that of the modern financial elite, who more often than not acquire wealth through exploitation and tax scams. For the Homeric hero in Greece, the scenario was very different. Faced with waring feudal chiefdoms and brutal combat, wealth was considered proof of success for the noble warrior, enhancing his prestige with each new conquest because it enabled him

15 Homer, *The Iliad*, 7.

16 The three Goddesses of Fate: Clotho, Lachesis, and Atropos.

to give valuable gifts to associates (*xeinoi*) and to reward followers, thereby ensuring their loyalty and dependency.[17] Through this accumulation of wealth, the tribal chiefdoms began to slowly transform into the *polis* and the State. Prior to this, there is no evidence for a separation of "classes" in Greece.

In the works of Homer, average citizens are sometimes also given the epithet *aristoi* (best), and they, too, are called "heroes."[18] Homeric warrior culture based on *areté*'s competitive standard was of great importance to the aristocracy's formation because all members of the community and their dependents, rich and poor alike, depended on the courage, strength, and skill of their fighting men.[19] According to Walter Donlan, the Homeric warrior's duty was to ensure that "responsibility and loyalty were directed towards his immediate family and the corporate household (*oikos*), extending outward to a small circle of friends and companions (*philoi, hetairoi*)."[20] It is from these small familial units that the aristocracy's foundations were laid.

---

17 Donlan, *The Aristocratic Ideal*, 4.

18 Ibid., 19.

19 Burns, *Organisation and Social Order*, 15.

20 Donlan, *The Aristocratic Ideal*, 23.

III. THE POLIS

THE POLIS, OR *civitas*, was a community of citizens who could be governed in various ways, depending on whether the governing element was a monarchy, oligarchy, democracy, or mixed constitution.[21] According to Vlassopoulos, "the *polis* is a composite thing, in the same sense as any other of the things that are wholes, but consist of many parts; it is, therefore, clear that we must first inquire into the nature of the citizen; for the *polis* is a *plêthos* of citizens, so that we have to consider who is entitled to be a citizen and what is a citizen."[22] It is of equal importance to discover what separated these citizens from the aristocrats, and why the *polis*' consent was required for them to govern.

In ancient Greece, the position of King belonged to the man who set up the city's hearth.[23] These kings would come to be known as *archons*.

---

21 Kostas Vlassopoulos, *Unthinking the Greek Polis: Ancient Greek History Beyond Eurocentrism* (Cambridge: Cambridge University Press, 2011), 19.

22 Ibid., 71.

23 Numa Denis Fustel de Coulanges, *The Ancient City: A Study on the Religion, Laws, and Institutions of Greece and Rome* (Kitchener, Ont: Batoche Books, 2001), 148.

Homer often depicts these kings as engaging in sacred rites. It is known from Demosthenes that the kings of Attica performed sacrifices, as well as from Xenophon, who writes that the kings of Sparta were the chiefs of the Lacedaemonian religion,[24] therefore suggesting a link between royalty and spiritual tradition.

The aristocracy's foundations emerged in the law of hereditary descent of the sacred fire, the right of primogeniture, and the right to pronounce the prayers, which was the prerogative of birth.[25] To a certain extent, the Homeric hero began to adopt both sacred and legislative functions in this transitive period between the early kingdoms and the later aristocracy. Hesiod chronicles this transformation of the Homeric warrior into aristocracy via his myth of the metals. This is the Greek equivalent to the Hindu cycle of yugas,[26] describing a progressive deterioration of society from a former glorious age toward an inevitable decline. This cycle is best thought of as a type of social entropy that eventually erodes all political systems, corrupting them via a steady stream of moral decay until they ultimately collapse from within. It is a painful reminder that nothing remains constant over time, for as Heraclitus reminds us, "everything is in flux." The myth of the metals presents civilization as a paradigm based on that of a living organism, extending from birth to death. The last age, where the aristocratic

---

24 Ibid., 355.

25 Ibid., 209-210.

26 A model of cyclic time, consisting of four ages, in which morality, spirituality, and quality of life progressively deteriorate.

principle[27] is finally destroyed, is the Iron Age. It is a time of sorrow that shares much in common with Hindu descriptions of the Kali Yuga, as described in Hesiod's *Works and Days*:

> Thereafter, would that I were not among the men of the fifth generation, but either had died before or been born afterwards. For now truly is a race of iron, and men never rest from labor and sorrow by day, and from perishing by night, and the gods shall lay sore trouble upon them.[28]

Plato later invokes the myth of the metals as told by Hesiod in the *Republic* to describe a caste system. Though all citizens are born from the earth, the guardian-rulers are described as golden, the military is silver, and the industrial and agricultural classes are bronze and iron.[29] Hesiod, however, inserts a "god-like race of *hero-men*" between the bronze and the iron race of his era, and these demi-gods (*hēmitheoi*) were the warriors who fought at Thebes and Troy, and now dwell in the Isles of the Blessed.[30]

Regardless of Hesiod's myth of the metals, one thing is clear: the definition of *areté* was not constant and changed just as the ages did. As Hellenic society became more structured and cohesive, less emphasis

---

27 The "aristocratic principle" denotes a time when the basis of good government was ethical and moral, prioritizing providing maximum happiness to all citizens. This, not the accumulation of wealth and power, is the true goal of political science.

28 Donlan, *The Aristocratic Ideal*, 30.

29 M. R. Wright, *Introducing Greek Philosophy* (Berkeley: University of California Press, 2010), 158.

30 Donlan, *The Aristocratic Ideal*, 30.

was placed on physical combat. Instead, leaders now focused on learning the art of politics and statecraft; skills involving rhetoric and persuasion were now required to convince the *polis* to go along with policy and legal decisions.[31] Friedrich Nietzsche lamented this transformation of the individual warrior's *agathos* into the rationalized *areté* of the classical *polis*, where the emphasis was placed merely on social politics. Presumably, Nietzsche's discontent stems from *areté's* transmutation into political values for the State, rendering it closer to the politics of the "herd" instead of pure individualism. Nevertheless, this represents a progression in political power's sequential development that is mandatory once a certain level of socio-cultural complexity is achieved. Under these conditions, the strongest individuals should be capable of adapting to the new requirements for leadership imposed by the *polis*' needs.

It is at this stage of civilization that politics first arises. By c.700 BCE, the political leadership of the early *polis* was in the hands of the "aristocrats" whose power base, as before, lay in their households (*oikoi*) and in the broader associations of lineage (*genos*) and *phratry*, which figure more prominently in the *polis* than in the earlier chiefdoms.[32] This created additional responsibilities for the aristocracy. Changes in military tactics also created new roles for the elite. In 700-650 BCE, there were alterations in the structure of army ranks which separated the more heavily-equipped aristocratic class from those with less military equipment, thus ensuring that

---

31 Wright, *Introducing Greek Philosophy*, 136.

32 Donlan, *The Aristocratic Ideal*, 38.

the aristocracy were the successors to the Homeric warriors whilst amalgamating this with their new political functions.

The mythical justification for this transformation was that "For want of political skill, Zeus sent Hermes to impart the virtues of *aidōs* and *dike* ('self-respect' and 'fair dealings with others' which together make up political *areté*)."[33] Zeus therefore created politics to ensure humanity's ethical behavior. At this point, politics is still equated with morality rather than social control. Justice (*dikaiosynē*), for example, was firmly associated with *areté*.[34] This is also apparent in Tyrtaeus' poems, where *areté* no longer means individual success and instead becomes *xynon esthlon* (the common Good) – a concept that does not appear in the epics.[35] The definition of *areté* shifts from the Homeric warrior's personal attainment to acts that benefit others. In a sense, it also represents a transition of the heroic from individual egoism to altruism for society. Werner Jaeger says that this is an attempt by Tyrtaeus to "recast the Homeric ideal of the single champion's *areté* into the *areté* of the patriot":

> It is important to stress that this is not so much a rejection of the code of the aristocratic warrior as it is a transvaluation. [...] Put another way, when the aristocratic *aretai* cease to command universal approbation, that is, cease to be functionally valuable, and if the aristocratic group wishes to retain its superior position in

33 Wright, *Introducing Greek Philosophy*, 157.

34 Donlan, *The Aristocratic Ideal and Selected Papers*, 68.

35 Ibid., 42.

> the community's regard, then it must seek other ways of demonstrating its superiority.[36]

This particular point by Jaeger draws attention to the essentially fluid nature of politics in general: unpopular ideas that prove stubbornly resistant to change are doomed to die. Aristocracy's defining characteristic is whatever quality is deemed desirable by the *polis* and not by the aristocracy themselves. In the Homeric era, it manifested as the warrior ideal. In the next phase, it was transformed into patriotism and statesmanship. Martial ability still plays a part, but individual combat and acts of heroism are now replaced by more significant battles that utilize strategic maneuvers. The aristocracy gained much greater power by successfully making the transition from warriors to military commanders and legislators.

Though usually conceived of as a city, the *polis* is neither an *ethnos* or a territorial region of dominion; in contrast with the medieval producer city, the *polis* is the form of the classical Greek State, which is a consumer city.[37] Each *polis* is more akin to a separate self-sufficient state. It was the expansion of the *polis* that created the need for increased legislation. To legitimize their position within it, some Athenian aristocrats now even pretentiously claimed to have traced their lineage back to divine ancestors or heroes.[38] This led to yet another transformation: aristocracy became

---

36 Ibid., 43.

37 Vlassopoulos, *Unthinking the Greek Polis*, 55.

38 Robin Waterfield, *Why Socrates Died: Dispelling the Myth* (New York: W. W. Norton & Company, 2009), 59.

hereditary. Status in life was now decided by birth alone, and those outside of aristocratic families could not challenge the right to rule. The distinction between *agathos*, "aristocrat" (defined in terms of bloodlines, wealth, and position) and *agathos*, "good man" (defined in terms of correct behavior) no longer existed.[39] Moral and ethical values were now presumed to have a hereditary or genetic component, and those lucky enough to be born into the aristocracy were believed to possess these qualities by virtue of inheritance.

This now created a third phase in Hellenic aristocracy where it parted with *aretê's* original meaning. The lower class was then automatically excluded from the possession of both power and morality. Only those born into the aristocracy were presumed capable of correct behavior and could lay claim to possessing *aretê*. Pindar attempts to justify these aristocrats' superiority by assigning them an almost mystical quality: the glory of the victor in his brief moment of triumph is the result of qualities inherited from past legendary heroes.[40] This is quite obviously an appeal to tradition[41] to legitimize bogus political authority. Education then also played a role in the distinction between aristocrats and non-aristocrats, with the Old Oligarch maintaining that it was the *dēmos*' lack of education and their

39 Donlan, *The Aristocratic Ideal*, 78.

40 Ibid., 98.

41 Political appeals to religion to substantiate spurious claims to authority were common even then; today they are so frequent it has become piteous to observe them in almost every disingenuous political movement seeking to use religion merely as an expedient tool.

poverty which led them to prefer a leveling of social differentiation.[42]

Physical appearance was another way to differentiate between aristocrats and others. They had adopted a different style of dress and hygiene, the second of which included keeping long hair, frequent bathing, and oiling.[43] Athenian aristocrats even went so far as to refer to themselves as *euatridai*, the "well-fathered," or *kaloi kagathoi,* the "beautiful and good."[44] This latter concept stems from Homer's notion that physical beauty (*kallos*) was connected with *areté*. This feature is absent in Hesiod, however, and in Homer's case his references may simply be literary embellishments that did not exist outside of poetic fiction. Indeed, Socrates, the aristocracy's most vociferous defender, did not make use of such concepts. Xenophanes likewise offers a description of the appearance of the aristocrats of his era:

> Having learned useless luxuries from the Lydians, while they were still free from hateful tyranny, they would go into the place of assembly wearing robes of all-purple – a thousand of them, no less – boastful, glorying in their well-dressed long hair, drenched with the perfume of elaborate scents.[45]

Descriptions such as this foretold the fourth phase of aristocracy in Greece: its downfall. Decadence had begun to set in with the removal of the requirement of merit, and the ease of the aristocracy's lifestyles

---

42 Donlan, *The Aristocratic Ideal*, 156.

43 Ibid., 161.

44 Waterfield, *Why Socrates Died*, 59.

45 Donlan, *The Aristocratic Ideal*, 53.

in turn led to apathy, which prevented them from performing their duties to the *polis*; thus, they had no way to demonstrate *areté*. Their social function had been eliminated. The entrenchment of biologically-inherited privilege created an inevitable decline of the aristocracy, who had very little left to do but ensure the day-to-day running of affairs and indulge in leisurely pursuits.

The aristocracy had mutated into an oligarchy based on wealth, which automatically excluded citizens who were not born into their ranks. By removing the requirement of merit, many aristocrats entered into a phase of decadence wherein they no longer felt obliged to be of service to the *polis*; in short, they began to embrace decadence and became redundant due to an excessively easy lifestyle. Like many of our modern politicians, they were born into wealth and never had to achieve anything on their own merit – which, instead of strengthening aristocracy, eventually crippled it. The age of entitlement for the elite was over; wealth was no longer deemed sufficient as an indication of superiority, and democracy was born. Aristocrats now struggled against democracy and faced a situation which Adkins describes:

> If one is a democrat in a democratic society and finds those who are traditionally held to be the 'best' citizens – i.e., men of wealth and good family – not to one's taste, the manner in which one will define the term *agathos* is clear. The cry must be 'It isn't what a man is that matters, but what he does.'[46]

[46] Ibid., 126.

Morality and ethics therefore became the contested battlefield for democrats and aristocrats to indulge in fierce debate. In this environment, democracy also had to fight, as it was faced with the problem of demonstrating that noble lineage and its inherent privileges were merely the results of luck. Phocylides was one of the first who directly attacked the notion of high birth as proof of value: "What good is noble birth (*genos eugenes*) for those who lack grace in words and counsel?"[47] Theognis also adopted this approach, saying that "Fate (*daimōn*) gives wealth even to the man who is completely worthless (*pankakos*), but to few men is given the measure of *areté*."[48] This sentiment also appears in Euripedes' *Electra*, where a common man is called *aristōs* due to his deeds and not by birth: "For this man is great (*megas*) among the Argives, nor puffed up by the reputation of a noble house, but, although he is numbered among *hoi polloi*, he has been found to be *aristōs*."[49] Sentiments such as this set the scene for a new form of aristocracy to compete with democracy for control.

---

47 Ibid., 68.

48 Ibid., 83.

49 Ibid., 150.

IV. DEMOKRATIA

DISSATISFIED WITH THEIR lot in life, the citizens of the *polis* devised a new system with which to address their issues with the aristocracy. This new system was to be called *demokratia* – meaning rule by the people. Together with monarchy/aristocracy, these are the two "mother constitutions" of all modern politics.[50] According to Plato:

> There are two mother-constitutions, so to speak, which you could fairly say have given birth to all the others. Monarchy is the proper name for the first, and democracy for the second. The former has been taken to extreme lengths by the Persians, the latter by my country; virtually all the others, as I said, are varieties of these two. It is absolutely vital for a political system to combine them, if (and this is of course the point of our advice, when we insist that no state formed without these two elements can be constituted properly) – if it is to enjoy freedom and friendship allied with good judgment.[51]

---

50 Aristocracy is called monarchy here because it is a derivative of the monarchical system.

51 Plato, trans. Trevor J. Saunders, *The Laws* (London: Penguin Books Ltd., 2004), 99.

The transition to full democracy in Greece was the product of a series of specific reforms by leading political figures such as Solon, Cleisthenes, and Ephialtes over the period stretching from the early 6th century BCE to the middle of the 5th century.[52] Democracy's rise in Greece was also aided by another form of government that few today would associate with it: tyranny. The *tyrannoi* (tyrants) were those who opportunistically grasped political power for themselves and attempted to establish family dynasties, playing on the discontent of the medium- and small-scale farmers, and masquerading as defenders and "champions of the people."[53] Instead of adopting the title of kings, they preferred to remains as "tyrants."

Tyrant here does not have the same meaning as it does today. A tyrant in the ancient Greek vernacular is a democratic leader who rules singularly in the same manner as a king, which is why Plato links tyranny to democracy and not aristocracy. What distinguished the tyrants from normal kings was the fact that they did not perform priestly duties and were merely political chiefs who owed their elevated status to force or election alone.[54] Hence why democracy precedes tyranny in Plato's works: without the support of the masses, a tyrant cannot come to power. For any sort of true dictatorship to occur, the complacency of the masses is required, which inherently implies that democracy is the perfect foundation for a tyrant to depose a king. When these democratic leaders come to wield the

---

52 Burns, *Organisation and Social Order*, 4.

53 Donlan, *The Aristocratic Ideal*, 39.

54 de Coulanges, *The Ancient City*, 150.

majority of power and establish their own hierarchy, they become tyrants. Unlike the aristocratic king, the tyrant comes to power with no credentials such as proven merit, skill, or ancestry; he comes to power via popularity and promises made to the citizens. Devoid of aristocratic honor, he has less of an obligation to keep these political promises.

In modern terminology, the tyrant is an unscrupulous political "populist." The issue Plato raises when he says that tyranny is the inevitable stage after democracy is to be understood in this context. The people are never truly in control - in democracy, a leader is still required and will arise - but the people choose him, and the people as a collective do not always make wise choices. Only the mode of selection is different; with the true aristocracy, it is by merit alone. With tyranny, it is a popularity contest based on stage theatrics and hyperbole. In theory, the reign of tyrants was an expression of the people's power, but in practice the tyrant ruled absolutely and with little regard for the common folk at all. Democracy therefore had many critics. The list is an impressive one, including Alcibiades, Critias, Thucydides, Socrates, Plato, Xenophon, Isocrates, Aristotle, and the anonymous author of *The Constitution of the Athenians* (the "Old Oligarch").[55] In his essay on Athenian democracy, for example, the Old Oligarch criticizes the social and political flaws in its premise:

> Any, he says, can hold office, and anyone who wishes can speak in assembly. In an even more pointed comment on equality he notes that

55 Waterfield, *Why Socrates Died*, 152.

> it would be better if they did not allow every citizen to speak or be a member of the Council (*boulē*) equally (*ex isēs*), but only the "cleverest" men (*dexiōtatoi*) and the *andres aristoi*; but democracy best suits and strengthens itself when the *ponēroi* are allowed to speak.[56]

The problem is that unqualified people came to exert influence over topics they had no knowledge or experience of. Furthermore, their claims were based not on expertise but merely on popularity and charisma, which led to the formulation of unsound policies. This was but one of many criticisms aimed at Athenian democracy. The classic refutation of democracy was that the masses were less educated and that, due to this, the people could not be trusted to select the best candidates. Other critics also felt that society's weaker members were oppressing them and that this enforced egalitarianism was unnatural. A further common rebuttal was that the people tended to favor the average candidates and, lacking knowledge of the topics involved, would elect candidates who possessed no qualifications at all over respected experts. The problem of unqualified people being empowered by Athenian democracy is described by M. I. Finley:

> The pivotal mechanisms were election by lot, which translated equality of opportunity from an ideal to a reality; and pay for office, which permitted the poor man to sit on the Council and on jury courts, or to hold office when the lot fell to him. [...] Though the pay was

[56] Donlan, *The Aristocratic Ideal*, 156.

> sufficient to compensate a man for the wages he might have lost as a craftsman, it was no higher than that. Hence no man could count on office-holding as a regular livelihood, or even as a better one for some periods of his life. […] In a sense, amateurism was implicit in the Athenian "definition" of a direct democracy. Every citizen was held to be qualified to share in government by the mere fact of citizenship.[57]

Other complaints about democracy were less specific and more concerned with policy and procedure. Large committees were also critiqued for inefficiency and overly bureaucratic procedures that wasted both time and money. With democracy, there were also problems with corruption in government and with the strong *philai*, those tightly-knit cartels that are always causing trouble.[58] By this time, however, democracy was no longer the dominant system, and as North says, "All the familiar aristocratic values had been thoroughly 'democratized' in fourth-century Athens." Politics had come full circle; it was now democrats who were *agathoi*, *sōphrones*, and *chrēstoi*, while aristocrats were *kakoi*, *ponēroi*, and *anandroi*.

---

57 Burns, *Organisation and Social Order*, 22.

58 Wright, *Introducing Greek Philosophy*, 171.

V. SOCRATES

THE MOST WELL-KNOWN critic of democracy was Socrates. Socrates was born circa 470 BCE[59] to Sophroniskos of the deme Alopeke, and he was around seventy years old when he died.[60] The setting of Plato's *Apology* is the trial of Socrates, where Meletus charged Socrates with impiety and corruption of the youth. These charges were presented to a jury c.399 BCE, who placed their verdict by secret ballot. Socrates was found guilty by the majority of the 501 jurors, sentenced to death, and executed.[61] Plato's *Apology* purports to be Socrates' initial speech for the defense.

According to Plato, all this happened before the beginning of the Peloponnesian War since Socrates is represented as resuming his mission after his return from Poteidaia.[62] The charges made

---

59 John Burnet, *Greek Philosophy: Thales to Plato* (London: Macmillan Press Ltd., 1978), 104.

60 Ibid., 103.

61 Robert Sherrick Brumbaugh, *Platonic Studies of Greek Philosophy: Form, Arts, Gadgets and Hemlock* (Albany: State University of New York Press, 1989), 227.

62 Burnet, *Greek Philosophy*, 110.

to indict Socrates were almost entirely bogus and quite obviously intended to silence his criticism of democracy. Socrates' political views start from a single premise: that "it was not those who held the scepter who were kings and rulers, nor those elected by unauthorized persons, nor those who were appointed by lot, nor those who gained their position by force or by fraud, but those who knew how to rule."[63] This single point serves to negate the claims of monarchy, oligarchy, democracy, and tyranny as legitimate constitutions in favor of a government by knowledgeable experts, and denies all claims to power by birthright, popularity, or other forms of entitlement. Socratic/Platonic aristocracy was not a return to the previous form of Hellenic aristocracy, but was intended to be a thoroughly new incarnation that was a fusion of the Homeric type with the need for specialized knowledge and statesmanship. In such a system, people rise to positions of authority simply by demonstrating their expertise or by receiving training from already existing experts.[64]

Judging from other historical references to Socrates, his peak of activity before the trial was in the 420s and 410s – meaning that the trial took place approximately twenty-four years after Aristophanes and Ameipsias had painted him as the most notorious atheist and subversive intellectual in Athens.[65] Aristophanes, a comic poet, even went so far as to portray Socrates as a villain in his comedy, *The Clouds*. For years this image persisted in the

---

63 Waterfield, *Why Socrates Died*, 176.

64 Ibid., 178.

65 Ibid., 192.

public mind, creating confusion between the real Socrates and his fictional representation.[66] It was an effective smear campaign for its era, and it had a lasting impact on public perception of Socrates.

Nonetheless, Socrates' influence had begun to expand. He had many followers, including the youth of the old aristocracy, those born into wealth and connected to the powerful families that had previously ruled Athens. One of the most cited of his admirers was Alcibiades, often depicted in satirical form as a young man infatuated with his much older teacher. Alcibiades is almost unanimously described as flamboyant, and at times even arrogant, which tends to obscure his actual personality and status. Alcibiades was by no means effeminate, and was a statesman in Athens as well as occupying prime military occupations. He was astute, outspoken, and well-connected to the old aristocracy; the State was as worried about him as they were Socrates. Thus, Alcibiades was undoubtedly not the foolish boy his enemies described him as, as can be seen from the following statement, where Alcibiades speaks of his exile:

> However, in the face of the prevailing political indiscipline (*akolasia*), we tried to be more reasonable (*metriōteroi*). There have been people in the past, just as there are now, who used to try to lead the masses (*ho ochlos*) into evil ways (*ponērotera*). It is people of this sort who have banished me. [...] As for *dēmokratia*, those of us with any sense at all (*hoi phronountes ti*) knew what it meant, and I as much as any...

66 Brumbaugh, *Platonic Studies of Greek Philosophy*, 229.

> but nothing can be said of a system which is a generally recognized foolishness (*anoia*).[67]

Sentiments such as this was widespread at the time. The younger members of the aristocratic class were among the first to be deprived of hereditary power by democracy. It was not Socrates' philosophy that rendered him politically threatening, but rather the identity of his followers and their connection to the old regime. Athens' democratic government feared that his students might revolt and push for a return to aristocracy. At Socrates' trial, this fear was disguised as the thinly-veiled offense of "corrupting the youth." Socrates defended himself against this allegation, saying:

> For this is the command to God, as I would have you know, and I believe that to this day no greater good has happened in the State than my service to the God. For I do nothing but go about persuading you all, old and young alike, not to take thought for your persons or your properties, but first and chiefly to care about the greatest improvement of the soul. I tell you virtue is not given by money, but that from virtue comes money and every Good of man, public as well as private. This is my teaching, and if this is the doctrine which corrupts the youth, my influence is ruinous indeed.[68]

---

[67] Donlan, *The Aristocratic Ideal*, 171.

[68] Plato, trans. Benjamin Jowett, *The Trial and Death of Socrates: Four Dialogues* (Mineola, N.Y.: Dover Publications, Inc., 1992), 30.

Here Socrates presents two points. Firstly, he has what can only be described as an anti-capitalist agenda, and secondly, he makes it clear that he perceives his mission as religious, not political. Socrates is on trial for both impiety and corrupting the youth; the two charges are connected, however. Socrates firmly believed that his actions came from a voice, or *daimon*, which advised him what to do. Socrates would often stand motionless for long periods of time in a trance-like state, communicating with a force referred to as his *daimon*. This *daimon* was primarily interpreted by Socrates as the word of God, but it was not a politically sanctioned mode of religious practice and therefore perceived as heretical by the State. The charge of impiety made against Socrates was not due to atheism but for rejecting the conventional mode of religious practice. Men had to conform to all the rules of worship and participate in all the processions and sacred acts. Athenian legislation punished those who failed to religiously celebrate any national festival by fining them.[69]

Socrates in no way perceived himself to be a criminal or a heretic. On the contrary, he was convinced that the Gods themselves directed his actions and that they all revolved around being good. According to Socrates, it was his moral duty to oppose the government because he believed he was the one destined to reform a grievously flawed political model. For Socrates, "doing good" meant acting as a social critic and questioning fundamental

---

69 de Coulanges, *The Ancient City*, 187.

Athenian beliefs.[70] Furthermore, Socrates clearly believed his fate was presided over by a higher divine power, as is evident here:

> If you put me to death, you will not easily find anyone to take my place. To put it bluntly (even if it sounds rather comical), God has assigned me to this city, as if to a large thoroughbred horse which because of its great size is inclined to be lazy and needs the stimulation of some stinging fly. It seems to me that God has attached me to this city to perform the office of such a fly, and all day long, I never cease to settle here, there and everywhere, rousing, persuading, reproving every one of you.[71]

One can conclude from this statement that Socrates is fully aware that he is a nuisance to the State, but he believes it is in their best interest for him to continue and "sting" the citizens as required. Intelligent people knew that the charges against Socrates were leveled to curb his influence over rebellious aristocrats, but since he could not legally be prosecuted for this, fallacious charges were manufactured. Socrates' actual crime in the eyes of Athens was that he created a new form of aristocracy that was palatable both to the public and the old aristocracy. Socrates took the aristocratic principle and revised it into a workable standard that was to be a form of government based on morality

[70] Josiah Ober, "Gadfly on Trial: Socrates as Citizen and Social Critic" in Christoper W. Blackwell, ed., *Dēmos: Classical Athenian Democracy* (The Stoa, 2003), 5, available at www.stoa.org/demos/article_socrates@page=1&greekEncoding=UnicodeC.html.

[71] Plato, trans. C. J. Rowe, *The Last Days of Socrates* (London: Penguin Books, Ltd., 2003), 57.

and *areté*. This idea automatically negated not just Athenian democracy, but the foundation of modern political science as we understand it today.

Socrates believed that only one who had attained a certain level of self-awareness was suitable to be entrusted with the governance of the *polis*, and that they must perform in an altruistic capacity instead of unadulterated self-interest, as is often the case with contemporary "career politicians." Socratic aristocracy borders on being anti-political, and it is quite clear that Socrates regards ethics as a matter of private conscience rather than social control.[72] Socrates also believed himself to be a teacher more than a political figure, and what he sought to teach was "the ideological bombardment of democratic education."[73] As he says in what follows, his goal was therefore to train individuals who would, after perfecting themselves, dutifully attend to attempting to perfect the State:

> Reflecting that I was really too honest a man to be a politician and live, I did not go where I could do no good to you or to myself; but where I could do the greatest good privately to every one of you, thither I went, and sought to persuade every man among you that he must look to himself, and seek virtue and wisdom before he looks to his private interests, and look to the state before he looks to the interests of the state; and that this should be the order which he observes in all his actions.[74]

72 Ober, " Gadfly on Trial," 6.

73 Ibid., 30.

74 Plato, *The Trial and Death of Socrates*, 36.

The emphasis is therefore on individual merit. It was not wealth or status Socrates was interested in, but an educated elite. He wanted a literal aristocracy, the "rule of the best," who were equipped to rule by their ability to know the good and how to make it happen.[75] *Crito* reiterates this, saying "that 'democratic knowledge' was tantamount to ignorance, [and] that it was a philosopher-citizen's duty to criticize ignorance," even if there were fatal consequences.[76] Socrates undoubtedly held a bleak perspective on politics in general. Under its sphere of influence, to truly fight for a right one must avoid political activism entirely or risk persecution:

> No man on earth who conscientiously opposes either your or another organized democracy and flatly prevents a great many wrongs or illegalities from taking place in the State to which he belongs, can possibly escape with his life. The true champion of justice, if he intends to survive even for a short time, must necessarily confine himself to private life and leave politics alone.[77]

Socrates believed that even the act of criticism or opposition under a democracy is enough to warrant execution. The State will invent approaches that make its disempowerment either difficult or futile. The only way to survive an attack by the State is to maintain a private station in the political arena. Presumably, this tactic is mentioned because a private citizen can

---

75 Waterfield, *Why Socrates Died*, 181.

76 Ober, "Gadfly on Trial," 17.

77 Plato, *The Last Days of Socrates*, 59.

engage in intellectual warfare while at the same time operating "beneath the radar." To be active in politics essentially means to draw the attention of the public to oneself – although a philosopher or any other creative type can gain influence by communicating with a select few, and the support of the masses is not required.

Antiphon once asked Socrates how he expected to teach others to be good at politics when he did not take part in it himself. Socrates replied, "Which would be the more effective way for me to take part in politics – by doing so alone, or by making it my business to see that as many people as possible are capable of taking part in it?"[78] This is why Socrates advises operating in private: to avoid or forestall an attack from the State just long enough to achieve the goal. Socrates did not seek success as a politician but instead as a teacher for future generations of political leaders. Socrates was prepared to martyr himself for this cause, even making use of his own execution to spread his philosophy:

> This all happened while we were still under a democracy. When the oligarchy came to power, the Thirty Commissioners, in their turn, summoned me and four others to the Round Chamber and instructed us to go and fetch Leon of Salamis from his home for execution. This was, of course, only one of many instances in which they issued many instructions, their object being to implicate as many people as possible in their crimes. On this occasion, however, I made it clear, not by my words but

[78] Waterfield, *Why Socrates Died*, 184.

> by my actions, that the attention I paid to death was zero (if that is not too unrefined a claim); but that I gave all my attention to avoiding doing anything unjust or unholy.[79]

It is evident that death is not Socrates' prime concern. Instead, he is avoiding "unjust" or "unholy" actions. At this stage of his life, Socrates is elderly, so death is imminent and inevitable. Misconduct is therefore a fate worse than death for him, as he prefers death to dishonor. This is of extreme importance for understanding Socrates' philosophy, for as he says:

> And what is that which is termed death, but this very separation and release of the soul from the body? [...] And the true philosophers, and only they, study and are eager to release the soul. Is not the separation and release of the soul from the body their especial study? [...] And when you see a man repining at the approach of death, is not his reluctance a sufficient proof that he is not a lover of wisdom, but a lover of the body, and probably at the same time a lover of either money or power, or both?[80]

A true Socratic philosopher does not fear death; on the contrary, he embraces it, because he believes in the purity of the soul and that the soul yearns to be free from the physical world. Despite being charged with "impiety," Socrates was clearly an immensely spiritual man who preferred to follow his own beliefs and not the mode of rigidly imposed worship

---

79 Plato, *The Last Days of Socrates*, 59.

80 Plato, *The Trial and Death of Socrates*, 64.

prescribed by the Athenian State. He sincerely believed his mission to be imposed on him by the Gods, referring to himself as the fellow slave of Apollo's swans.[81] For Socrates, the body was a prison of flesh that bound the higher self and prevented unity with the divine:

> The lovers of knowledge are conscious that their souls, when philosophy receives them, are fastened and glued to their bodies: the soul is only able to view existence through the bars of a prison, and not in her own nature; she is wallowing in the mire of all ignorance; and philosophy, seeing the terrible nature of her confinement [...] shows her that this is visible and tangible, but that what she sees in her own nature is intellectual and invisible.[82]

Whether fated by the Gods or not, Socrates had no choice but to accept his death sentence or be revealed as a hypocrite before the people of Athens. The trial forced him to demonstrate his belief in the soul. He could not accept the dishonor of clinging to life and supporting what he perceived as unjust, nor could he admit fear of death, because he had described it as the ultimate freedom of the soul. Judging from the general direction of his dialogue, one has to consider the prospect that Socrates may even have intended martyrdom for himself from the outset. It is undoubtedly clear that he used the publicity surrounding his trial as a platform to promote his philosophy, and that he used his execution to

---

81 Burnet, *Greek Philosophy*, 110.

82 Plato, *The Trial and Death of Socrates*, 81-82.

posthumously deliver a fatal wound to Athenian democracy.

When examined from Socrates' perspective, however, there was little else he could do without surrendering his principles, and he saw no reason why they should be surrendered.[83] This is expressed in his prophetic statement below, which he intended to be self-fulfilling:

> And now, O men who have condemned me, I would fain prophesy to you; for I am about to die, and that is the hour in which men are gifted with prophetic power. And I prophesy to you who are my murderers, that immediately after my death punishment far heavier than you have inflicted on me will surely await you. Me you have killed because you wanted to escape the accuser, and not to give an account of your lives. But that will not be as you suppose: far otherwise. For I say that there will be more accusers of you than there are now; accusers whom hitherto I have restrained: and as they are younger, they will be more severe with you, and you will be more offended at them. For if you think that by killing men, you can avoid the accuser censuring your lives, you are mistaken; that is not a way of escape, which is either possible or honorable; the easiest and noblest way is not to be crushing others, but to be improving yourselves. This is the prophecy which I utter before my departure to the judges who have condemned me.[84]

---

83 Plato, *The Last Days of Socrates*, 38.

84 Plato, *The Trial and Death of Socrates*, 39.

The prophecy of Socrates did, in fact, come true. His most famous student, Plato, more than adequately accepted the challenge and influenced the course of philosophy for two millennia after his teacher's death. If Plato is to be regarded as the "father of Western philosophy," then one must consequently acknowledge Socrates as its godfather. Socrates, to his credit, does not blame the citizens for his fate and merely states that it is natural for the average man to understand and fear a philosopher because they deal with ideas beyond the average man's comprehension:

For I deem that the true disciple of philosophy is likely to be misunderstood by other men; they do not perceive that he is ever pursuing death and dying; and if this is true, why, having had the desire of death all his life long, should be repine at the arrival of that which he had always been desiring and pursuing?[85]

Here again, Socrates implies that death and the separation of the soul from the body are the true philosopher's goals. As he notes here, these "true philosophers" who eagerly embrace death are rare, drawing a comparison between the mystics of the Elysian Mysteries and the study of philosophy: "For 'many,' as they say in the mysteries, 'are the thyrsus-bearers, but few are the mystics,' meaning, as I interrupt the words, the true philosophers."[86]

Socrates' execution was performed purely to protect the power of Athenian democracy, but by ordering it they also posthumously empowered Socrates beyond their wildest nightmares. The specter of Socrates has haunted democracy well into

---

85 Ibid., 61.

86 Ibid., 67.

the modern era. Plato, following Socrates' lead, makes it clear that the government will pass laws to ensure the current leaders are protected, and that its regime will be perpetuated by marginalizing, ostracizing, or punishing its critics: "So do you imagine, they say, that when a democracy has won its way to power, or some other constitution has been established (such as dictatorship), it will ever pass any laws, unless under pressure, except those designed to further its own interests and ensure that it remains permanently in power?"[87] In the case of Socrates, his opinion, being contrary to that of democratic Athens, was enough to have him sentenced to death, but his accusations live on, as recorded by Plato:

> If you expect to stop denunciation of your wrong way of life by putting people to death, there is something amiss with your reasoning. This way of escape is neither possible nor creditable; the best and easiest way is not to stop the mouths of others, but to make yourselves as well behaved as possible. This is my last message to you who voted for my condemnation.[88]

As already pointed out, to a certain extent Socrates chooses to play the role of a martyr and go down fighting in the name of his cause. Like the old Homeric aristocrats, he does not fear death, only dishonor, saying that "the difficulty is not so much to escape death; the real difficulty is to escape from wickedness, which is far more fleet of foot."[89]

---

87 Plato, *The Laws*, 125.

88 Plato, *The Last Days of Socrates*, 68.

89 Ibid., 67.

Socrates had to be dying for some purpose if the conduct leading to his death were to be seen as good, honorable, and just.[90] Beliefs such as this were frequent during his lifetime, and it was generally assumed that there were five cardinal virtues: wisdom, moderation/temperance, bravery, justice, and piety. These virtues were thought to be necessary to perform well and enable one to live the "good life" as a whole. Possession of these virtues was the precondition for attaining happiness (*eudaimonia*), which allowed one to live a good life. These virtues were also linked to the attainment of excellence in any given field, and therefore to both *areté* and *timé*.

The idea that the virtues were skills was extensively developed in the early Platonic dialogues, especially in *Gorgias,* where Socrates argues that moral virtues are skills.[91] The principle of *eudaimonia* is one exclusive *telos* (end) of the *areté* (virtue) of *theoria* (contemplation of the divine). The intellectual virtues, whatever they are, function to maximize the production of *eudaimonia*.[92] Happiness and the "good life" are thus intrinsically wed to spirituality and virtue. The philosopher's virtue also introduces wisdom (*phronesis*), however; the philosopher is expected to brave dangers and sacrifice pleasures to obtain wisdom.[93] The philosopher therefore endures an intellectual battle that is similar to that of the Homeric warrior, for as Azsacra Zarathustra says,

90 Ibid., 102.

91 Paul Bloomfield, "Virtue Epistemology and the Epistemology of Virtue" in *Philosophy and Phenomenological Research*, Vol. LX, No. 1 (January 2000), 24.

92 Ibid., 32.

93 Plato, *The Last Days of Socrates*, 107.

"Danger is the initial condition of the philosopher." Plato even provides us with an example of a Socratic prayer that illustrates the intellectual asceticism that a philosopher should aspire to:

> Dear Pan and all gods here, grant that I may become beautiful within and that my external possessions may be congruent with my inner State. May I take wisdom for wealth, and may I have just as much gold as a moderate person, and no one else, could bear and carry by himself.[94]

Socrates, despite his best efforts to transcend the physical world, remains a mortal and also has flaws. Like the heroes of the Greek tragedies, Socrates is afflicted with the terrible problem of *hybris.* Ironically, Alcibiades, known for his own arrogance, points this out when he says, "You are a *hybristes*, Socrates. If you deny it, I will produce witnesses." Alcibiades repeats this specific charge three times and peppers his speech with references to Socrates' scorn (*kataphronesis*) and arrogance (*hyperephania*).[95] *Hybris* is a hazard for those who exhibit *areté*, and it is the root of the destruction of the heroes, Gods, Titans, and philosophers alike - via narcissism, arrogance, pride, and vanity. Thus, even possession of the virtues is paradoxically enough to preclude one from attaining virtue. The philosophical fall from grace due to *hybris* is described by Will Desmond:

---

94 Waterfield, *Why Socrates Died*, 42.

95 Will Desmond, "The *Hybris* of Socrates: A Platonic 'Revaluation of Values' in the *Symposium*" (Dublin: Yearbook of the Irish Philosophical Society, 2005), 43.

The *hybris* of the new philosophical 'aristocrat' is not brought out by wine or power, but by insight into an order that transcends any individual; transcends even the temporal realm. Tempered by such enlightenment, this new philosophical *hybris* is *hybris* in the sense that it rises from a tremendous intellectual energy, and expresses itself in the relative dishonoring of conventional values, and of conventional people.[96]

[96] Ibid., 63.

VI. ARETÉ

IF HYBRIS CAUSES the fall of heroes, then it is by *areté* that they arise. The concept of *areté* is crucial to understanding the ideas of Socrates and Plato, and through them, the aristocratic principle. In Socrates and Plato, *areté* is a universal but non-essential part of human nature, and people differ in the degree of *areté* they possess.[97] *Areté* undergoes a specific transition in their works, taking on an ethereal aspect and becoming a virtue. This makes the task of providing a definition even more difficult. What exactly is virtue? Can virtue be taught, or is it part of an individual's psychological composition, and therefore an innate genetic trait? Neither Socrates nor his predecessor Plato had to contemplate the prospect of genetically-transmitted virtue and moral qualities as we do today, given our advancements in biological sciences. Nor did they have to answer whether personality was the product of nature or nurture. They could only work with logic to search for an answer, and neither philosopher believed that *areté* (as a virtue) could be taught. Virtue is explained as:

---

97 Plato, trans. W. K. C. Guthrie, *Protagoras and Meno* (Harmondsworth: Penguin Books, 1956), 31.

> [...] what makes one a member of the community. Everyone has some virtue, and he has got it through teaching, which started in babyhood and continues throughout life. To ask who are the teachers of it is like asking who has taught you to speak your native language.[98]

This implies that virtue is an innate social skill akin to Victor Turner's use of *communitas.* It is a type of social intelligence derived from naturally-occurring social bonds. This, however, is a more complex theory. Though virtue is learned, it seems that the capacity for it is innate and that the capacity for an individual's virtue differs in proportion to that of others. Socrates appears to believe that virtue cannot be taught past its natural capacity and states this to Protagoras.[99] However, when Meno asks Socrates how virtue is acquired, whether by instruction or in some other way, Socrates replies that he cannot answer because he does not yet know what it is, saying that "The fact is that far from knowing whether it can be taught, I have no idea what virtue itself is."[100] While virtue is a characteristic, it is obtusely resistant to definition, dwelling on a plateau of unique abstraction, even for Socrates. Protagoras points out that even great statesmen are sometimes unable to pass on their virtue to their sons, so he also decided that virtue cannot be entirely hereditary. Virtue therefore begins to take on a metaphysical existence, with Socrates concluding that it must be a kind of intuition or a type of wisdom, saying that

98 Ibid., 32.

99 Ibid., 51.

100 Ibid., 125.

it merely comes to a man "by divine inspiration without taking thought."[101] Socrates then proceeds to elaborate further:

> If then virtue is an attribute of the spirit and one which cannot fail to be beneficial, it must be wisdom; for all spiritual qualities in and by themselves are neither advantageous or harmful by the presence with them of wisdom or folly. If we accept this argument, then virtue, to be something advantageous, must be a sort of wisdom.[102]

According to Socrates, *areté* is both a virtue and a form of wisdom. From this, one can conclude that the form of aristocracy he advocated is based on excellence in wisdom and virtue, with exemplary morality functioning as the observable evidence of the right to govern. Socratic aristocracy is therefore "ethical politics." The idea put forward is that democratic political science presupposes no formal qualifications for government. For all other occupations, one is trained in order to gain employment - but for government, there is no training and no certified accreditation. Socrates thus concludes that, subconsciously, the skills required for politics cannot be formally taught, as he outlines below:

> Now when we meet in the Assembly, then if the State is faced with some building project, I observe that the architects are sent for and

[101] Ibid., 106.

[102] Ibid., 142.

> consulted about the proposed structures, and when it is a matter of shipbuilding, the naval designers, and so on with everything which the Assembly regards as a subject for learning and teaching. If anyone else tries to give advice, whom they do not consider an expert, however handsome or wealthy or nobly-born he may be, it makes no difference: the members reject him noisily and with contempt, until either he is shouted down and desists, or else he is dragged off or ejected by the police on the orders of the presiding magistrate. [...] But when it is something to do with the country that is to be debated, the man who gets up to advise them may be a builder or equally well a blacksmith or a shoemaker, merchant or shipowner, rich or poor, of good family or none. No one brings it up against any of these, as against those I have just mentioned, that here is a man who without any technical qualifications, unable to point to anybody as his teacher, is yet trying to give advice. The reason must be that they do not think this is a subject that can be taught.[103]

Socrates' ultimate conclusion is therefore that the types of specialized knowledge which cannot be taught are wisdom and virtue, and that these are the two most important qualities for a potential leader. The ideal leader is thus skilled in both: a philosopher. In consequence, Socrates offers a third way between aristocratic and democratic politics as his Athenian audience understood them; essentially, this is the practical dimension of Plato's philosopher-kings, or

103 Plato, *Protagoras and Meno*, 50-51.

what Micheal S. Kochin calls "academic politics."[104] According to this view, politics is a game of flattery and propaganda, "not an activity suitable for refined, 'beautiful people,' or for real men."[105] One must also understand that philosophy, in this context, relates to a highly educated group: Athens' top intellectuals. The reign of "philosopher-kings" does not necessarily imply philosophy as we understand it today, but all the academic disciplines — *the sciences as well as the humanities*. According to Socrates, the philosophers (and/or intellectuals) must be compelled to govern. His alternative to democracy is an aristocracy based on intelligence, wisdom, and education rather than wealth or birthright. Plato best describes this with his ship-of-state metaphor:

> Imagine the following situation on a fleet of ships, or on a single ship. The owner has the edge over everyone else on board by virtue of his strength, but he's rather deaf and short-sighted, and his knowledge of naval matters is just as limited. The sailors wrangle with one another because each of them thinks that he ought to be the captain, despite the fact that he's never learnt how. They're forever crowding closely around the owner, pleading with him to entrust the helm to him. They think highly of anyone who contributes towards their gaining power by showing skill at winning over or subduing the owner, and describe him as an

104 Michael S. Kochin, "Academic Politics: Between Aristocracy and Democracy" in *Political Research Quarterly* (University of Utah, 2011), 247.

105 Ibid., 251.

> accomplished seaman, a true captain, a naval expert; but they criticize anyone different as useless. They completely fail to understand that any genuine sea-captain has to study the yearly cycle, the seasons, the heavens, the stars and winds, and everything relevant to the job, if he's to be properly equipped to hold a position of authority in a ship. In fact, they think it's impossible to study and acquire expertise at how to steer a ship or be a good captain. When this is what happens onboard ships, don't you think that the crew of such ships would regard any true captain as nothing but a windbag with his head in the clouds, of no use to them at all?[106]

Only a properly skilled captain can control the ship, but spurred on by belief in absolute equality, the owner is challenged, not by those who can do the task better, but because each individual believes they have an equal right to do his job. The crew fights each other for power, but none of them seek to gain the knowledge that renders them fit to control the ship. Narcissism overrides wisdom, endangering not only the owner but the whole ship. From this point of view, politicians are portrayed as a group of power-hungry incompetents eager for control at any cost but unable to fill the role of the experienced and educated leader.

As painful as the idea may be, too much freedom paves the way for egoism wherein everyone believes he is entitled to an equal quantity of power simply by virtue of his existence. For all other essential positions, there are formal requirements;

[106] Plato, *The Last Days of Socrates*, 176-177.

not so for politics. The most critical roles in the State have the least formal requirements. This is the crux of the argument: by leaving the arena of politics open to all and the voting open to people who do not have the correct information to select the best candidate, politicians are appointed who are incompetent, and who might possibly even damage the *polis*. The following rule of logic applies: mediocre men produce mediocre States, bad men produce bad States, but the Socratic leader appointed because of personal excellence will create an excellent State. The State and the government are the mirrors of the man who leads.

The Ideal is therefore an aristocracy composed of virtuous qualified experts, and a meritocracy of mind and spirit. His alternative to democracy is thus an educated and intelligent elite that bypasses the idea of class. To Socrates, the successful pursuit of any occupation demanded the mastery of particular knowledge, a skill, or a technique, and this was true above all of the direction of the city's affairs, on which the happiness of the citizens necessarily depended.[107] The principle and *raison d'etre* of a State is to be sought not in mediocrity, but excellence, and it is not by its average that a nation is measured, but by its genius.[108]

Plato also entwines this idea with Hesiod's myth of the metals to ascribe social roles within the State. All members are born from the earth, but with

---

107 Plato, *Protagoras and Meno*, 14.

108 P. H. Frye, "Plato's Political Ideas" in *The Mid-West Quarterly*, Vol. II, No. 1 (October 1914), 11.

different mixtures of gold, silver, copper, and iron.[109] In an obvious analogy to this, Plato likewise divides the possible systems of government into five distinct groups: "the first is a monarch, typically accompanied by an aristocracy, the second a timocracy, or an aristocracy of talent, the third an oligarchy, the fourth a democracy, and, finally, a tyranny."[110] As the quality of the ages declines, so does the quality of government and the individual merits of rulers.[111]

---

109 Patricia M. Lines, "Shackling the Imagination: Plato and Rousseau on Education" in *Humanitas*, Vol. XXII, No. 1 & 2 (The Center for the Study of Statesmanship at The Catholic University of America, 2009), 47.

110 Alexander Jacob, *Nobilitas: A Study of European Aristocratic Philosophy from Ancient Greece to the Early Twentieth Century* (Lanham, Md.: University Press of America, 2001), 6.

111 Lines, "Shackling the Imagination," 47.

VII. PLATO

PLATO WAS SOCRATES' most famous student and diligently continued his teacher's work. His real name may have been Aristocles, but the nickname Plato, meaning broad, was given to him either because of his broad physique or perhaps because of his wide-ranging intellectual pursuits. He was born in 427 BCE to an aristocratic family during a period of social and political unrest following the outbreak of the Peloponnesian War. In 404 BCE, the "Thirty Tyrants" overthrew the government and instituted a short-lived reign until democracy was restored in the same year. This included two of Plato's uncles: Critias, the leader of "the regime of the Thirty Tyrants," and his fellow junta member Charmides.[112] Because of this, the danger Plato and Socrates presented to the political order was very real. Socrates' trial marked the end of Plato's political ambitions, however, and he left Athens to continue studying philosophy. Plato did not solicit the public as Socrates did and confined his work within the Academy, thus avoiding the problems that plagued Socrates.[113]

---

112 Kochin, "Academic Politics," 249.

113 Ober, *Gadfly on Trial*, 24.

The vast majority of Plato's ideas on the nature of God have their ideological roots in Socrates' teachings. Both Plato and Socrates drew comparisons between the order in the cosmos and the nature of the divine, applying these correlations to ideas such as justice and the human soul. Because order is beneficial, they connected it to God, arguing that because order is evident in nature, it implies the work of an intelligent creator. One example of this line of reasoning is found in *Timaeus,* where it describes how the good, order, and justice are represented in nature, stating that if we follow the life of virtue, we shall also be following the natural order and thereby be better off than if we go against nature. The order that is presented in nature is the essence of God and the Ideal. *Critias* takes this idea even further, illustrating how the citizens of Plato's ideal city will, given the natural order's support, overcome even the greatest of challenges. Ultimately, this is also how Athens surpassed the decadence and disorder found in its opposing city, Atlantis. In relation to order and the principle of the good, Athens sustained itself through what Socrates and Plato refer to as the mystical quality of virtue.

Both *Timaeus* and *Critias* describe a world in which Good and order are evident in everything from the motions of the planets to human society. This order, according to Plato, filters down from the realm of the Ideal to the physical world. The material world is thus penetrated by the Ideal, which produces a direct intermingling of the transcendent world of ideas and the world of the senses. Without this intervention, the cosmos would exist in a state of disorder, as both chaotic and evil. Because the nature of order and the Good permeates all that exists unless it is inherently abnormal, it follows that the same pattern is found in humans and in the soul. "The Form of the Good" is the organizing principle of the world of Forms. From textual references, several conclusions can be drawn about this:

> This idea appears in *Phaedrus* where souls are named as the origin of movement. This idea is further developed in *Timaeus*. The soul, as the origin of movement, acts as an intermediary between the eternal world of Ideas and the material world. Human morality is therefore connected to the order of the cosmos, for just as humans possess a soul, so too is there a soul of the world. Because of this, changes in the physical world appear first in the world of Ideals and Forms and are connected to the divine.[114]

Man, by virtue of this connection, is a part of the cosmos. As a creature of order and civilization, he is first and foremost a member of the city or *polis*. This separates him from other animals, and man evolves accordingly to become a *zoon politikon*. The cosmic order has replicated itself from the macrocosm of God to the organization of the *polis*, and man's part in the cosmic order is simply to adhere to it and fulfill the cosmic plan while furthering the *polis*' growth. Thus, the *Republic* reflects the conviction that the proper function of "political science" is to design an ideal state.

Even Plato's fictional accounts are intended to have an impact on the material. Socrates in the

[114] Brumbaugh, *Platonic Studies of Greek Philosophy*, 71.

Republic says that a person rules "in his own *polis*, but perhaps not in his native land except by divine providence." Glaucon interprets this *polis* as the Ideal (and thus internal) Kallipolis, which Socrates affirms, saying it exists in heaven, and that by this model the philosopher-king establishes a "political regime" in his own soul.[115] The city remembered in the Socratic discourse would thus be "a paradigm laid up in heaven" and one that is "nowhere on earth."[116] The *Republic* consequently reflects the conviction that the proper function of "political science" is to design an Ideal state and to decide what is "good for human life" through an enlightened legislator who can choose among various combinations of policies.

Additionally, it suggests that by creating an Ideal one can evoke it such that it becomes a physical reality, which means that Plato *prescribes* rather than *describes* a "utopia." This demonstration of the right way to develop political science also postulates the form mimicking the Ideal.[117] Plato's most famous depiction of this is in the *Republic*. This theme also recurs in the dialogue *Laws*, however, which provides the blueprint for a fictional city to be founded in Crete, in accordance with the general custom of a legislator.[118] This city is to be named Magnesia, and its guiding principles are:

A. that certain absolute moral standards exist;
B. that such standards can be, however

---

115 Ober, *Gadfly on Trial*, 31.

116 John Sallis, *Chorology: On Beginning in Plato's Timaeus* (Bloomington: University of Indiana Press, 1999), 30.

117 Ibid., 132.

118 Wright, *Introducing Greek Philosophy*, 174.

imperfectly, embodied in a code of law;

C. that most of the inhabitants of the State, being innocent of philosophy, must never presume to act on their own initiative in modifying either their moral ideal or the code of laws which expresses it.[119]

The *Republic* thus presents the theoretical Ideal, whilst *Laws* is essentially the *Republic* modified after it has been created in the physical world.[120] The *Statesman* forms a bridge between the *Republic* and *Laws*, wherein a fully qualified ruler lays down the laws that bring the new utopia into existence, acting as a magician who takes the Ideal and transcribes it through his will into the physical realm. The context of *Laws* is, accordingly, different from earlier works. Moreover, although it makes use of earlier themes, it is in fact a new development in Plato's thought; Trevor J. Saunders implies that in it, the importance of law now holds supremacy:

> Plato now sees law as the supreme, though essentially imperfect, instrument for the moral salvation of society: he calls it the 'dispensation of reason', and the entire life of the community must accordingly be governed by a detailed code of laws which will express as far as possible the philosopher's vision of the true Good.[121]

According to Plato, the world of Ideals could influence the world of Forms, so it is reasonable to conclude that these laws are necessary to evoke the

---

119 Plato, *The Laws*, xxxiv.

120 Ibid., xxxiii.

121 Plato, trans. Trevor J. Saunders, *The Laws*, xxxii.

polis in the external world of Forms. Socrates' Ideal city, the Kallipolis, would therefore be presided over by philosopher-kings whose unique access to the Ideal of the Good gives them the required knowledge to rule in a maximally just fashion, and this is a necessary requirement for a utopia to be actualized in the physical world of Forms. It is enacted not to control the population, but to maximize *eudaimonia*, the good life, for all citizens. The *Republic* is an inner, perfect *polis*: the spiritual city[122] — which, only once it is perfected at the conceptual level, can be externalized.

Robert Sherrick Brumbaugh affirms this, saying that "The *Republic*, despite its title and history, is best described as a treatise on value theory and on theory construction in the social sciences, not as a political or psychological tract."[123] This kingdom of the Good can only be imagined and actualized by men who have already perfected the Good in themselves. Its politics are not based on wealth, but instead on virtue and *areté*. Plato's political Ideal is consequently predominantly a spiritual one that reverses the order of priority between matter and soul, as is seen in the following:

> Physical motion, he argues, is always produced by some antecedent motion. But what started the process? It can only be soul, the one thing capable of self-generated motion (look at animals, who move themselves: we say they are "alive," that is, they have a soul).[124]

---

122 Frye, "Plato's Political Ideas," 3.

123 Brumbaugh, *Platonic Studies of Greek Philosophy*, 25.

124 Plato, *The Laws*, 366.

According to Plato, it is the actions of the soul that precede action or causality in the physical world. Thus, the soul is the first cause and therefore the catalyst for creating physical activity in the material world, acting as an intermediary between the Ideal and the Form. This attitude is expressed even more clearly in the following passage, which places the soul above the appetitive and material desires:

> Every man directs his efforts to three things in all, and if his efforts are directed with a correct sense of priorities he will give money the third and lowest place, and his soul the highest, with his body coming somewhere between the two. In particular, if this scale of values prevails in the society we're now describing, then it has been equipped with a good code of laws.[125]

For that reason, the soul is the key to understanding Plato's utopia. The whole point of legislation for Plato was to maximize happiness for the citizens via a codified set of instructions on morality. From this perspective, it is immediately apparent that almost every form of government in existence falls short of fulfilling Plato's primary objective.[126] Plato concluded that the only hope for society lay in removing government from the ignorant hands of mediocre men so that the State could be directed according to the findings of philosophy:[127]

125 Ibid., 167.

126 Ibid., 165.

127 Ibid., xxix.

> The philosopher-ruler contemplates the values as they actually are (*phusei*, 'in their nature') in the Forms, and cannot resist trying to reproduce them in his own soul. Thus he becomes as well ordered (*kosimos*, a significant epithet) and godlike as a man can be [...] Then he turns, however reluctantly, to his duty as statesmen and stamps these same characteristics on the citizens, who thus poses *dēmotikē areté* – the result, not of episteme on their part, but merely of right opinion.[128]

The State's qualities are thereby reflections of its leaders. As much as the moral ruler imprints his citizens with good qualities, the same can be said of a bad leader in terms of bad qualities. Because politicians all seek material power first rather than knowledge, they are automatically regulated to a lower plane than philosophers as far as morality is concerned. This is Plato and Socrates' gambit – not that philosophers are entitled to leadership, but simply because their moral nature makes them better leaders. It is akin to the old paradox that whoever seeks power the most should automatically be excluded from possessing it. The fundamental error of Athenian politics was not the system itself, but its inversion of values wherein the lower appetitive qualities were given dominance over the higher ones. As Alexander Jacob says:

> The legislators of the land must govern with a full knowledge of the spiritual constitution of man, that is, the rational and passionate

128 Donlan, *The Aristocratic Ideal*, 177.

> elements that Plato had discerned in the soul. It is the duty of the legislators to ensure the predominance of the higher aspect of the soul over the lower.[129]

There is little doubt that Socrates was the Ideal teacher for Plato. Certainly, Socrates lived an extended "life" as an Ideal, whether Plato intended him to bear this function or not. It is even possible that Plato deliberately refashioned the historical Socrates into his fictional Ideal, hoping that someone would emulate him in the physical world of Forms. Socrates, whether by intent or accident, is Plato's 'Ideal' of the philosopher-king.

---

129 Jacob, *Nobilitas*, 9.

VIII. THE STATE

IN THE REPUBLIC, Plato identified the four virtues within the population as being divided into three classifications: the Perfect Guardians, the Auxiliary Guardians, and the "Third Class."[130] This is similar to – but not identical with – the *varṇa* (caste) system of India:

> Wisdom guides the philosopher-ruler. Courage moves the auxiliaries (the soldiers and the bureaucrats). Discipline, sometimes translated as moderation, assures that each class carries out its assigned role and that the governed obey the governors. Finally, justice – the supreme ordering principle – ensures harmony and balance within the individual and the State.[131]

Regarding the Perfect and the Auxiliary Guardians, Frye believes that "these two classes taken together form an aristocracy; there is no doubt about it, they are the superiors of the third estate in every respect."[132] "Superior" is not an appropriate term, however,

130 Plato, *The Laws*, xxx.

131 Lines, "Shackling the Imagination," 44.

132 Frye, " Plato's Political Ideas," 7.

for these two classes were purely meritocratic; their roles do not provide a privileged lifestyle, but involve rigorous social duty and responsibility. Their members are closer to practicing devout asceticism than they are "privileged" in any manner. Their main purpose is to serve society, and not vice versa. As such, the roles were of necessity allocated to those who would work for the betterment of others despite receiving very few rewards. This idea is further explicated in *Laws*, where Plato writes:

> And the proper basis is to put spiritual goods at the top of the list and hold them – provided the soul exercises self-control – in the highest esteem; bodily goods and advantages should come second, and third, those said to be provided by property and wealth. If a legislator or a state ever ignores these guidelines by valuing riches above all or by promoting one of the other inferior goods to a more exalted position, it will be an act of political or religious folly.[133]

The ideal ruler has no interest in materialism and even renounces it to perform his social function. It is not a matter of "privilege," but instead that the philosopher-king *has no desire to be privileged*, and this is one of the qualities that separate him from other men. The incorruptible philosopher-king, who presumably attained his position by being virtuous, is required to be immune to all forms of temptation, be they in the form of wealth, sex, or power. The distribution of justice is a rational art or science

[133] Plato, *The Laws*, 104.

demanding both natural aptitude and acquired skill.[134] As such, the dispenser of justice must be highly self-disciplined. A taste for materialism denotes a particular weakness of character, which exposes the *polis* to the risk of corruption. For justice and the Good to preside, virtue and honor must be maintained.

The central tenant of the *Republic* is therefore not that "good consequences . . . follow from being just, but because justice itself is so great that nothing gained by injustice could be greater."[135] Justice and goodness are innate characteristics in all citizens of such a State, even the wrongdoers. The *Republic* upholds the Socratic paradox that "No one does wrong willingly," and asserts that all crime is involuntary, in the sense that the criminal has been "conquered" against his "real" wishes by ignorance, anger, bad education, or pernicious environment; a "cure" rather than punishment is thus required.[136] In this regard, the justice system is different from that which operates today: instead of focusing on discipline, the premise is that crime is a behavioral disorder that can be cured, and the perpetrator is then considered to require rehabilitation. In circumstances where the criminal cannot be cured, however, the death penalty is advocated – providing evidence that even in a Socratic utopia, some citizens remain so flawed that their very existence is too dangerous to be tolerated.

---

134 Frye, " Plato's Political Ideas," 11.

135 Brendan Boyle, "Platonic Thoughts" in *The Wilson Quarterly*, Vol. 31, No. 4 (Fall 2007), 107.

136 Plato, *The Laws*, xxxvii.

Timaeus deals with the presence of flaws in society, taking this concept of integral justice and ethics one step further when it draws a comparison between the State of Athens and the corruption inherent in Atlantis:

> The *Timaeus* shows how the good order of justice and goodness, in general, is represented in nature, such that if we follow the life of virtue, we shall also be following the natural order and thereby be better off than if we go against nature. The *Critias* further shows how citizens of Socrates' ideal just city will, given the support of the natural order, overcome even the greatest of challenges. So we see in the victory of ancient Athens over Atlantis a practical demonstration of how the world – that is *Timaeus*' world of good order – will sustain the efforts of the virtues.[137]

As much as Athens is presented as the virtuous State, Atlantis is depicted as its polar opposite. Brumbaugh says that it is clear "that Plato meant his Atlantis to be a blueprint of a bad society, eventually corrupted by prosperity, disorganization, and a lack of education, just as surely as he meant his other cities in the *Republic* and *Laws* to be models of good order."[138] Whether Atlantis was an actual city or Plato's fictional creation, Atlantis is intended to be Athens' mirror image. The differences between the two are even present at their conception. Athens, of course, is virtuous and founded by the virgin Goddess

---

137 Plato, *Timaeus and Critias*, x.

138 Brumbaugh, *Platonic Studies of Greek Philosophy*, 116.

of Wisdom, Athena. Atlantis, on the other hand, was founded by the fecundity of Poseidon.[139] Plato therefore draws a distinction between them, with Athens as a projection of the intellectual/spiritual and Atlantis being based on the lower material/appetitive desires.[140] The sea that surrounds Atlantis represents exposure to the corruptive influence of money and luxuries.

Laws makes this point explicit: "[Being situated by the sea] fills the land with wholesaling and retailing, breeds shifty and deceitful habits in a man's soul, and makes the citizens distrustful and hostile, not only among themselves but also in their dealings with the world outside."[141] The decadence inherent in Atlantis lies in its "appetitive" function, which links it to the physical desires instead of the higher intellectual or spiritual ones. Atlantis' attractive outward appearance also makes it more dangerous and deceptive to those who cannot see past its illusionary facade. This is contrasted with the spirit of Athens, which draws on the Goddess Athena's characteristics:

> The Goddess founded this whole order and system when she framed your society. She chose the place in which you were born with an eye to its temperate climate, which would produce men of high intelligence; for being herself a lover of war and wisdom she picked a place for her first foundation that would produce men most like herself in characteristic.[142]

139 Ibid., 117.

140 Plato, *Timaeus and Critias*, xxvii.

141 Ibid., xxviii.

142 Ibid., 15.

As with other traditions, especially those of the Vedic, Hellenic Tradition draws on notions of cosmic order, bound and decreed by the patterns in nature and the mystical nature of the Moirai, or Fates, an influential group of figures similar to the Norse Norns. This Triad of Goddesses primarily functioned similarly to the significantly less anthropomorphized Vedic Triad of *ṛta/dhārman/karman*. The ideal microcosm of human society therefore follows a similar teleological pattern to that of the macrocosm.[143] An inclination towards order and justice is as pre-programmed into human behavior as it is in the division of cells, planets' orbits, and the seasons' changes. For *Timaeus* the first principle of cosmology is a teleological one: it refers to the Good that the cosmos is organized to possess.[144] In this regard, it is an inherently organic political system. As Alexander Jacob writes, "the state is not an organization that was installed by artificial convention (*nomoi*), but rather one that arose naturally (*physei*) as a result of the desire to achieve social conditions that would enable man to live the 'highest life' possible."[145] This has obvious parallels with the concept of political science's proper role being the pursuit of the goal of *eudaimonia* and the quest for *areté*.

---

143 "As above, so below."

144 Plato, *Timaeus and Critias*, xix.

145 Jacob, *Nobilitas*, 10.

IX. CONCLUSION

THE OTHER GREAT philosopher to express concern about democracy was Aristotle, the tutor of Alexander the Great. Aristotle's influence on Alexander the Great is directly responsible for Alexander's cultural achievements, which were equally as impressive as his military ones. Aristotle continues in a very similar pattern of thought to that of Socrates and Plato, using the term "virtue ethics" as an extension of theories on *areté*. Aristotle defines *eudaimonia* as "an activity of the soul according to complete excellence/virtue over a complete life."[146] He also says that "The virtue of man is the state of character which makes a man good and which makes him do his own work well."[147]

Aristotle's political analysis of constitutions reached similar conclusions to those of Plato and Socrates, stating that there were only three forms of

[146] Bahadır Küçükuysal & Erhan Beyhan, "Virtue Ethics in Aristotle's Nicomachean Ethics" in *International Journal for Human Sciences*, Vol. 8, No. 2 (Singapore, 2011), 45.

[147] Ibid., 48.

politics: rule by one (monarchy), few (aristocracy), or many (democracy).[148] Though Aristotle agrees that *areté* is derived from intellectual and moral merit, he believes that virtue can be taught via a process of learning by repetition. As Hugh Mercer Curtler states, "This latter quality is called 'moral virtue' by Aristotle, and it is primarily a matter of conditioning – what Aristotle calls 'habit' or 'disposition' (*éthos*)."[149]

Looking further at Aristotle's treatment of virtue ethics, it is composed of two distinctive elements:

> Virtue ethics treat areatic notions, such as "good" or "excellence," rather than deontic notions, such as obligation, ought, right, and morally wrong. In pointing out the difference between virtue ethics and modern moral theories, Slote (2000) stresses that most modern ethical theorists believe "rightness as a matter of producing good results or conforming to moral rules or principles, but virtue ethics specify what is moral in relation to such inner factors as character and motive."[150]

Virtue ethics concentrates on man's internal processes before the external social implications which follow. This organic model of the State – the "*teleological politica*" – is similar to the classical theist argument for the existence of God. Organic

[148] Wright, *Introducing Greek Philosophy*, 171.

[149] Hugh Mercer Curtler, "Can Virtue Be Taught?" in *Humanitas*, Vol. VII, No. 1 (The Center for the Study of Statesmanship at The Catholic University of America, 1994), 44.

[150] Küçükuysal & Beyhan, "Virtue Ethics in Aristotle's Nicomachean Ethics," 44.

politics follow patterns in nature, however, whereas the politics of artifice operates in contradistinction to itself. According to Aristotle, the natural mode for humanity is to be a social, and hence political animal: "From these, it is evident that the *polis* is part of the natural order (*tôn physei esti*) and that man is by nature a political animal, and a man that is by nature and not by fortune citiless, is either an inferior human or above humanity."[151] Those who can live without the social elements of human nature found in civilization are thereby either below the norm or above it. Aristotle describes the varied constituents within the *polis*' social framework:

> For we agree that every *polis* possesses not one part (*meros*), but several [...] One of these parts (*mere*) therefore is the *plêthos* of people which are concerned with *trophê*, the so-called peasants, and second is what is called the *banausoi*, the mechanic class; and third is a commercial class, and fourth is the class of manual labourers, and the fifth class is the one to defend the *polis* in war [...] and the class also plays a part in judicial justice, and in addition to these the deliberative class, deliberation being a part of political intelligence [...] and a seventh class is the one that offers liturgies (services) to the community by means of its property, the class we call the rich. And an eighth is the class of public servants, that is those who serve in the magistracies, inasmuch as without rulers, it is impossible for a polis to exist.[152]

151 Vlassopoulos, *Unthinking the Greek Polis*, 77.

152 Ibid., 72.

Aristotle recognizes that individuals have different professions, and that such a "class" system is inevitable, whether it exists officially or unofficially. What is essential, however, is that the system's existence maximizes the good life for *all* citizens instead of detracting from it. Regardless of minor differences in theory between Plato and Aristotle, it was Aristotle who ended democracy in Greece via educating Alexander of Macedon, the God-King. Without this education, Alexander would never have been able to conquer Greece and the lands beyond.

In some ways, the Ideal of aristocracy also overlaps with a more recent philosophical opponent of democracy, Friedrich Nietzsche. As Burnet says, "The worship of the strong man or 'hero,' who can rise superior to all petty moral conventions – in fact, of the 'superman' – seems to have been fostered in the fifth century BC by much the same influences as in the nineteenth century AD."[153] This occurs precisely because aristocracy in fact exists as an immortal Ideal. Nietzsche's aristocratic radicalism was a resurgence of this form of aristocracy, but it was published in an age when democracy was fully entrenched. Nietzsche's brand of aristocracy thus differs from both the Hellenic form and that which we now call a constitutional monarchy. Had aristocracy kept to either Hellenic or Nietzschean philosophy and not regressed to a system based merely on wealth and birthright, it would still be able to exist as a functioning political system. Instead, the very conditions that brought the aristocracy to power – personal merit, wisdom, virtue, honor, and excellence – were abandoned and taken for granted.

153 Burnet, *Greek Philosophy*, 98.

The same problems which crippled the aristocracy in Ancient Greece now gnaw away at the heart of democracy today. Like aristocracy, democracy could become an oligarchy, but instead of emphasizing the well-being of citizens, the emphasis is now on capital gain – *the value structure is inverted.* Modern democracy could become an oligarchy based on economics rather than an opposing form based on society. These flaws are most evident in American politics, for, as Alexander Jacob states:

> The reason for this, to some, rather alarming fact, is that it is completely impossible to base a government on the vote of the masses that are altogether disparate in their understanding and mastery of the principles of politics and ultimately conduct themselves as though politics were a system of hectic compromises to be achieved through base bargaining – and profit-making – in every sphere of social action. While it may be argued that the professional politicians that actually supervise the final stages of policy-making are indeed quite experienced in the art of politics, it is clear that no politician which rises to power on the opinion of a mostly unlearned majority can be truly reliable, let alone admirable.[154]

A similar statement is made by Ogochukwu Okpala, who also voices the concern that not all individuals in democracies possess the intellectual skill with which to recognize the best candidates, writing that "the average individual may not have the wisdom

154 Jacob, *Nobilitas*, 2.

to be involved in the appointment of a leader and second, potential leaders' abilities should be carefully and objectively scrutinized before nomination."[155] Furthermore, John Dunn writes that democracy has resolved itself into two quite distinct formulations,

> one dismally ideological and the other fairly blatantly Utopian. In the first, democracy is the name of a distinct and very palpable form of modern State, at the most optimistic, simply the least bad mechanism for securing some measure of responsibility of the governors to the governed [...] In the second, democracy (or as it is sometimes called participatory democracy) is close to meaning simply the good society in operation, a society in which [...] all social arrangements authentically represent the interests of all persons, in which all live actively in and for their society and yet all remain as free [...] roughly as they could urgently and excusably desire.[156]

According to this statement, modern democracy either does not in actuality exist, or it is merely the least offensive form of government available. Neither of these two definitions are palatable. An effective political system should be *desirable.* No ideology is eternal, and what destroys all of them is the profound inability to fulfill their primary function – promoting the "good life" as far as is possible for all citizens. The

---

155 Ogochukwu Okpala, "Plato's Republic vs. Democracy" (n.d., Neumann University), 54. Available at silo.tips/download/plato-s-republic-vs-democracy.

156 Burns, *Organisation and Social Order*, 1.

lower the satisfaction of the citizens, the greater the risk of political instability, which stems from the common man's discontent and the consequential annulment of his consent to be governed.

PART II

VEDIC TRADITION
&
THE ARTHAŚĀSTRA

The Principle of Divine Sovereignty in India

The subsistence of mankind is termed *artha*, wealth; the earth which contains mankind is *artha*, wealth; that science which treats of the means of acquiring and maintaining the earth is the *Arthaśāstra*, Science of Polity…

– Cāṇakya, *The Arthaśāstra*

I. INTRODUCTION

THE ROLE EARLY political models play in shaping future civilizations has been severely underestimated. In recent times, however, the works of Georges Dumézil have been examined in regards to his tripartite theory of society amongst the Indo-Europeans. This is merely the tip of the proverbial iceberg for a much more inclusive and lesser-studied system of power which arose in India, to become one of the greatest empires in human history. There is a distinct sequential progression of thought from the Mitra/Varuṇa model espoused by Dumézil to the *Laws of Manu* and on into the Mauryan Empire. This reaches its apex of sophistication in the famous text known as the *Arthaśāstra* (or *Arthaśāstram)*, which was only rediscovered by the West in the early twentieth century.

The *Arthaśāstra* is essentially a political instruction manual for the aspiring *Cakravartin* (World Emperor) to govern effectively, and also functions as a treatise on military strategy. The author, commonly known as Cāṇakya (also known as

Kauṭilya or Vishnugupta), is one of the most elusive figures in history. Not only was his life mythologized, he was also so skilled at subterfuge and political misdirection that some experts doubt Cāṇakya even existed. As the advisor to Chandragupta, who successfully conquered and united India in order to forge an empire by following the instructions in this text, Cāṇakya is in effect the ultimate "man behind the curtain," ruling vicariously through his pupil, Chandragupta. Frequently referred to by academics as the "Indian Machiavelli," Cāṇakya is perhaps also the most ruthless political strategist in human history, with experts often declaring that he makes "Machiavelli look harmless."

Despite Cāṇakya's often harsh tactics, the *Arthaśāstra* demonstrates a natural development from early Vedic political ideas right through to models of power in contemporary Buddhist and Southeast Asian political science. The *Arthaśāstra* therefore provides a link from early Vedic thought through to the modern world, where it continues to be studied in defense, military theory, and politics. In economics, it is currently viewed as a possible solution to the modern crippled economy. Despite this, those outside of the academic world remain oblivious to the existence of this immensely important text due to its relative obscurity among the English-speaking audience. Quite possibly the most dangerous political treatise ever composed, the *Arthaśāstra* stands unique as the only successful instruction manual for global conquest in existence. Moreover, the book combines spiritual and religious philosophy with politics to create the being known as the *Cakravartin*: the King who is also a spiritual leader.

Judging from the Mauryan Empire's history, it would seem that this use of religious motifs was not just strategic and that Cāṇakya, despite his often underhanded strategies, really did believe in the *Arthaśāstra*'s spiritual elements and was not just using them as a political ruse. To verify this, one can easily see that Chandragupta was a devout Jain,[1] and Aśoka the Great,[2] who followed him, was the royal patron of Buddhism and a key figure in the success of Buddhism as a religion. Thus, not only was Cāṇakya influenced by Vedic religion, the emperors themselves proceeded to spread religious thought through their respective reigns, propagating his legacy throughout India and Asia. Because of this, there is an unbroken line of political and traditional power running directly from the Indo-European past, through the *Laws of Manu*, to Cāṇakya, and continuing into Buddhism.

---

[1] Chandragupta Maurya renounced the throne around the third century BCE and became an ascetic under the Jain saint Bhadrabahu, migrating south with them and ending his days in *sallekhana* (death by fasting).

[2] Aśoka Maurya is referred to as Samraat Chakravartin Aśoka, the "Emperor of Emperors Aśoka." *Aśoka* means "painless, without sorrow." In his edicts, he is referred to as Devānāmpriya (Pali Devānaṃpiya, or "The Beloved of the Gods") and Priyadarśin (Pali Piyadasī, or "He who regards everyone with affection"). Under Aśoka's rule, divine kingship was modified into a Buddhist form which can be seen even today in parts of Southeast Asia.

II. VARUNA

THE EARLIEST REFERENCES to political power in India harken back directly to the ancient past, where they are referenced in texts surrounding the enigmatic god Varuṇa. Varuṇa is an ancient deity, with history hiding much of the figure's symbolism and worship. Etymology suggests that the name "Varuṇa" stems from the root "v" or "var," meaning "to cover," "to screen," "to veil," "to conceal," "to hide," "to surround," or "to obstruct" in the *Rig Veda*, and also "to ward off," "to check," "to keep back," "to prevent," "to hinder," or "to restrain" in the *Atharva Veda*.[3] These terms present a level of abstraction which suggests that Varuṇa occupied a position of prominence in Vedic tradition.

Surviving textual descriptions of Varuṇa indicate that he was a god with strong solar connections, which are evident in his iconography. In literary depictions Varuṇa is bald and of a

[3] Rohana Seneviratne, "Varuṇa, the Guardian of Morality in the Rgveda" in C. S. M. Wickramasinghe, ed., *Philologos: Essays Presented in Felicitation of Merlin Peris*. (Colombo: Godage International, 2008), 269-311.

fair complexion, with yellow eyes and a face that resembles Agni, shining like fire. Furthermore, he is portrayed as a mature man clad in golden ornaments. This imagery immediately conjures to mind a solar deity. However, some images by *brāhmaṇa* differ from descriptions of Varuṇa in the *avabhtha* or the sacrificial bath of the *Aśvamedha* sacrifice described as an obscure figure called Jumbaka or Jmbaka with a white (śukla) body, bald head, protruding teeth (*viklidha*), and with a reddish-brown hue.[4] These texts were possibly composed at a time when early Vedic influences were on the wane. New modes of religious thought were entering Hinduism which were created to disempower earlier Vedic ideas.

Varuṇa's golden eyes are associated with the Sun in particular, with Varuṇa himself conceived of as "all-seeing": with his eyes being the "eyes" of the Sun, Varuṇa observes all as he chooses. This ability to see everything that transpires also earned him the epithet of being "thousand-eyed." The golden and solar descriptions are far more common than those describing Varuṇa as old or of a reddish-brown hue. It seems likely that detractors introduced these less flattering descriptions as the role of the Vedic gods diminished in Hindu society.

Before his popularity waned, Varuṇa occupied a prominent role in Hinduism. He was referred to with an extensive range of titles such as

---

4 Ibid.

deva-gandharvas,[5] divaukas,[6] King of nāgas,[7] an asura, and "The King of the Gods and The King of Both Gods and Men," or "The King of the Universe."[8] Varuṇa is repeatedly referred to as the universal monarch (*samrāj*), and while this term is also applied to Agni and Indra, it is applied to Varuṇa nearly twice as often as it is with Indra.[9] According to the *Śatapatha Brāhmaṇam,* Varuṇa is thought of as The Lord of the Universe, with a throne amid heaven; neither the birds nor the rivers can reach the limit of his dominion.[10] In several instances Varuṇa is also called *dhtavrata* (one who maintains the fixed rules of conduct), and even the gods themselves do not violate his unbreakable laws or ordinances, called *vratani.*[11] The attribute of sovereignty (*kṣatra*) is also used in connection with Varuṇa, and the term "ruler" (*kṣatriya*) in four of its five occurrences refers to Varuṇa or the Ādityas, and only once to the gods

---

5 A demigod.

6 Sky-Dweller.

7 A mythological serpent being, identified with a cobra or hooded serpents. There is some evidence to show that the classical form of the nāga as mythological beings rises from a very old *kṣatriya* clan in Vedic times who had the cobra as their symbol, and that this ancient clan gradually became incorporated into myth and symbolism; many of the "naga" referred to in myth may in fact represent historical figures. The *Mahābhārata* (The Great War) also relates the story of the origin of a conflict between Garuda the Sun Bird and the nāga people, which possibly relates to the lineage of bloodlines in the epic.

8 Seneviratne, "Varuṇa," 311.

9 Arthur Anthony Macdonell, *Vedic Mythology* (Honolulu: University Press of the Pacific, 2004), 24.

10 J. Gonda, "Ancient Indian Kingship from the Religious Point of View," in *Numen*, Vol. 3, Fasc. 1. (January 1956), 62.

11 Seneviratne, "Varuṇa," 269-311.

in general.[12] These aspects are further illustrated via his titles and their etymological interpretations as related by Rohana Seneviratne:

> Varuṇa is entitled to a large number of attributive names in the *Rig Veda* such as '*samrat*' or the universal monarch, '*svarat*' or the independent ruler, '*kṣatra*, *kṣatriya*' or king, '*mayin*' or the upholder of the occult power alias *maya* or the crafty, '*dhtavrata*' or the ordinances-bearer, '*nitidhara*' or the rules-bearer etc. On his royalty or sovereignty the honorific epithets *samrat*, *svarat* and *ksatra* are ascribed while *mayin*, *dhtavrata* or *nitidhara* are those emphasizing his role in maintaining and promoting morality. '*Putadakṣa*' or the one who has purified thoughts, '*sukratu*' or the great intellect are due to his admirable characteristics.[13]

Varuṇa also wields the great occult power of *māyā*,[14] which is a reference to his strength to bind others by magic and illusion. It is by Varuṇa's power and ordinances that the Moon moves through the heavens and the Sun rises; as the solar deity par excellence, his power is greater than that of his twin Mitra, who only reigns during the light of day. Varuṇa, by contrast, is the lord of light by night *and*

---

12 Macdonell, *Vedic Mythology*, 24.

13 Seneviratne, "Varuṇa," 269-311.

14 From the Sanskrit "*ma*" (to create), meaning magic, supernatural power, and the binding of others to the world through illusion (in this regard it also has a strong sexual connection, with the power to fascinate through the intoxication of the senses).

day. Mitra is the god only of the celestial light of day.[15] Though they are nearly inseparable in early Vedic thought, a clear demarcation between the two deities was later introduced with the *Taittirīya Saṃhitā* (VI, 4, 8) which states that:

> "This world had neither day or night, it was (in this respect) non-distinguished"; the gods said to the couple Mitra-Varuṇa (dual form *mitrāvaruṇau*) "Make a separation!" Mitra produced the day, Varuṇa the night. (*Mitro'har ajanayad Varuṇo rātrim*).[16]

This is more of an explanation of natural phenomena than anything else, with the *Rig Veda* itself taking on a henotheistic tone. Mitra is the visual aspect of the Sun, and Varuṇa is the non-visual aspect, in a similar way to Savitṛ, who also possesses a similar solar and abstract description. By his association with night and his solar imagery, it is reasonable to conclude that Varuṇa is not the atmosphere or the night sky, but instead the Sun when it can no longer be perceived – the time at night when the Sun rises in the opposite hemisphere. As Varuṇa diminishes, Mitra becomes visible, and therefore it is Varuṇa who takes on more mysterious qualities, such as the power of magic and of *māyā*. Mitra, by contrast, is visible; his aspects are visible, while those of Varuṇa are not. The separation referred to is therefore the rising and setting of the Sun, with Mitra as the "Golden Sun" and Varuṇa

---

15 Macdonell, *Vedic Mythology*, 25.

16 Georges Dumézil, trans. Derek Coltman, *Mitra-Varuna: An Essay on Two Indo-European Representations*, (New York: Zone Books, 1988), 77.

becoming the "Hidden Sun." Varuṇa is represented as the more powerful of the dyad. The three heavens and the three earths are said to be under his control. Before the separation referenced above, Mitra is inseparable from Varuṇa in both the *Rig Veda* and the *Atharva Veda*. All the *Rig Veda* hymns dedicated to Mitra are also dedicated to Varuṇa.[17] When Mitra and Varuṇa were together, they ruled in tandem, as lords of *ṛta* (cosmic order), sometimes being called guardians of order (*ṛtasya gopā*), or the observers of order (*ṛtāvan*).[18]

In terms of their use in a political sense, Georges Dumézil's classic text *Mitra-Varuna* describes them as a dual model of sovereignty, with Mitra being the sovereign under his reasoning aspect: luminous, ordered, calm, benevolent, and priestly; and Varuṇa as the sovereign under his belligerent aspect: dark, inspired, violent, terrible, and warlike.[19] This does not seem correct, however, for Varuṇa is not depicted as being tyrannical. In the original texts, Varuṇa is the deity who was sent to punish the wicked, but was also regarded as merciful, and the faithful easily averted his wrath. Dumézil may have altered the description deliberately, as he did with Odin, to discourage specific interpretations of his texts.[20] Varuṇa punished those who transgressed the *ṛta* or the *dharma* (the human order). Through *māyā*, Varuṇa binds the universe to his will as the supreme

---

17 Ibid., 66.

18 Macdonell, *Vedic Mythology*, 25.

19 Dumézil, *Mitra-Varuna*, 72.

20 Dumézil altered some of his texts to prevent National Socialist interpretations of them being made, and this is deliberate on his part.

possessor of occult power, ensuring that the social order's rules and regulations are obeyed. Because of this, Varuṇa is also the god who punishes humans, binding and fettering them with his noose (*pāśa*). His wrath is aroused by sin and the infringement of his ordinances, and the fetters with which he binds sinners are often mentioned as being sevenfold and threefold, ensnaring the man who tells lies and passing by he who speaks the truth.[21] It is worth noting that the notion of "sin" as being associated with the power of *māyā* persists into contemporary Hindu religious thought. The sin itself arises from transgressing *ṛta*, of which *dharma* or *dhārman* is only the human reflection. In this role Varuṇa has no connections with death or the afterlife, however, which was presided over by Yama, who metes out legislation and punishment in the afterlife just as Varuṇa does for the living.

[21] Lying was considered to be a serious transgression of the moral order in Vedic society. Macdonell, *Vedic Mythology*, 25.

III. SOVEREIGNTY & TRADITION

BECAUSE OF HIS TERRIBLE wrath and all-seeing eyes, Varuṇa is conceived of as a sovereign deity who is both omniscient and omnipresent. His primary concern is to ensure that humans maintain a moral code, setting down the foundations of *ṛta* and *dharma* that underlay the functional nature of the cosmos and humanity's role within it. Varuṇa is the protector (*tasya gopa*), observer (*kha tasya*), and promoter (*tāyu*, *tāvat*) of order, and although Agni operates as a second protector, Varuṇa's prominence is much greater.[22] Varuṇa's duty as the universal sovereign of the cosmic and human order is to ensure that the laws of both are upheld, introducing a legislative model of governance into the Vedic tradition via religion that eventually became the paradigm for other Indo-European political and state models.

Indra is another Vedic deity with a special connection to sovereignty, who is more personalized in myth than Varuṇa and much less abstract. The

22 Seneviratne, "Varuṇa," 269-311.

importance attributed to Indra is evident in the fact that around 250 hymns celebrate his greatness, more than those devoted to any other god – almost a quarter of the total hymns in the *Rig Veda*.[23] Like Varuṇa, he sees all and is referred to as a universal monarch or a self-dependent sovereign who is said to reign (*eka*) by his might as an ancient seer.[24] Like Varuṇa, Indra, too, is an upholder of the cosmic order and is accredited with a natural bent towards the destruction of evil, enemies of gods, and enemies of mankind [25]

Of the three deities cited as an early model for the sovereignty function in Vedic thought, the names ascribed to Varuṇa seem to indicate that he was the supreme power, eclipsing that of even Mitra, who remained powerless at night; Varuṇa, on the other hand, initially presided over both night and day. The boundary which separated them seems to have been established at a much later point. Varuṇa represents the Sun, which is active at night – the rising and setting Sun that moves between night and day, thus establishing a dyad similar to that of Dionysus and Apollo. Though Indra is commonly regarded as the King of the Gods, this seems more like the role of an earthly king, with Varuṇa as the cosmic ruler or celestial monarch. Thus, the model of sovereignty in the Vedic era lends itself towards a solar model of power and not the Jupiterian model offered by Indra.[26] This model of sovereignty will be evident

---

[23] Macdonell, *Vedic Mythology*, 54.

[24] Ibid., 58.

[25] Gonda, "Ancient Indian Kingship from the Religious Point of View," 62.

[26] Indra is the equivalent of Zeus and Jupiter.

once it manifests in the material world of Hindu polity via the figure of the *Cakravartin*, or universal ruler.

Sovereignty in Hindu thought begins with the Ārya, or noble caste. Contrary to popular thought, it is not a racial term. This is made evident by the texts themselves, which repeatedly emphasize that to be an Ārya, actions are accorded prominence over ethnicity. This was modified later as the castes, or *varṇa*, divisions were reconstructed in India. The term *kṣatriya* became the new title for both the military caste and the aristocracy. It is the *kṣatriya*, not the *brāhmaṇa*, who control the legislative function and are the protectors of the people and the law. Similar descriptions are made of kings who are said to protect the Earth with the force of their two arms. This is an obvious reference to their *varṇa*, as the *kṣatriya* caste is born from the two arms of Puruṣa, the cosmic man. Various rulers are in fact called *dīrghabāhu* (of long arms), *mahābāhu* (of mighty arms, long-armed), or *vipulāṃśo mahābāhur mahoraskaḥ* (broad-shouldered, long-armed, broad-chested).[27]

The role of *rājan* (king) was also sometimes explicitly limited to a *kṣatriya*.[28] For example, in the *Mahābhārata* the term for "member of the military class," *kṣatriya*, is said to mean the following: "He saves from destruction." A similar explanation of the word already occurs in the *Bṛhadāraṇyaka Upaniṣad*, which describes the *kṣatriya* as "nobility" and proceeds to say, "Behave like the sun which protects (*pāti*) and destroys all creatures by its

27 Gonda, "Ancient Indian Kingship from the Religious Point of View," 40.

28 Ibid., 37.

rays."[29] Likewise, in the *Mahābhārata* Arjuna's role as a *kṣatriya* is to protect the people, which, as the section known as the Śrīmad Bhagavad Gītā relates, this is the *dharma* appropriate to his *varṇa*; "Every *kṣatriya* who advances against the enemy in battle takes part in the sacrifice of battle (*yuddhayajña*)."[30] The *Śāntiparva* even goes so far as to say, "a *kṣatriya* in distress should take (by force) what he can, with a view to (ultimately) protect the people."[31] This effectively permits the *kṣatriya* to break the *dharma* itself, but only to uphold the safety and prosperity of the Kingdom and the people.

It is erroneous to associate the *brāhmaṇa varṇa* with complete dominion over the Vedic tradition's magico-religious sphere, for the *kṣatriya varṇa* not only had its own method of achieving *mokṣa* (as related by the principle of detachment, which Krishna relates to Arjuna in the Śrīmad *Bhagavad Gītā*) the King or ruler also functioned as a spiritual leader and embodiment of the *dharma*. Throughout Hindu thought, there is a widespread reverence for authority and an association between authority and supernatural power. The King and priests are associated with the regulation of meteorological processes and other natural forces.[32]

---

[29] Ibid., 37-38.

[30] Torkel Brekke, "The Ethics of War and the Concept of War in India and Europe," in *Numen*, Vol. 52, No. 1 (Netherlands: Brill, 2005), 70.

[31] Sarvepalli Radhakrishnan & Charles A. Moore, *A Sourcebook in Indian Philosophy* (Princeton, N.J.: Princeton University Press, 1989), 166.

[32] Gonda, "Ancient Indian Kingship from the Religious Point of View," 44.

Sacrifice is explicitly called one of the King's duties, and "worshiper" is a well-known epithet which reflects the King's association with the preservation of *dharma*. Only a corrupt king would redirect the sacrifices meant for the gods to himself,[33] an act which would portray the King as both *anārya* and *anṛta* (ignoble and acting against the cosmic order). Like the priest, the role of the King is as a defender of the sacred and a mouthpiece of the gods: "The king and the priest uphold the moral order in the world" (*dhṛtavratau*). The first stanza of a well-known work on the elements of polity, the *Kāmandakiya-nītisāra*, is also very significant: "By whose might (majesty, dignity, power: *prabhāva*) the world is established on the eternal (*śāśvata* – "what has always been") path, that god (*devaḥ*) is victorious (*jayati*), prosperous and illustrious (*śrīmān*), administering justice (*daṇḍadhāra-*, lit. "rod-bearer"), lord of the earth."[34]

In the Vedic tradition, the King is *dharmātman*, an embodiment of *dharma*, and by upholding *dharma*, the ruler becomes *rāṣṭrabhṛt* (a sustainer of the realm), which is considered to be the King's most important duty.[35] This *dharma* is the ruling power of the *kṣatriya varṇa* (*ksatrasya ksatram*), and it explicitly states that there is nothing higher than *dharma*: "So a weak man can defeat a strong man by means of justice as one does through a king."[36] Likewise, though some may debate about who held the real reins of power in India, and whether it was the *brāhmaṇa* or the *kṣatriya*, it is clearly stated in the ancient texts that

33 Ibid., 50.

34 Ibid., 53.

35 Ibid., 53-54.

36 Ibid., 55.

the King can commit brahmanicide, and that this act could be atoned for by performing an *aśvamedha*.[37] The *Laws of Manu* do not permit a *brāhmaṇa* to kill a King, so the priests and the sovereigns are definately not on equal footing. The King, unlike the priest, is not just the mouthpiece of the gods. He is viewed as being almost of divine origin himself. The King's divine power is attested to by the fact that he may not stand on the earth with bare feet, a restraint no doubt intended to prevent his mystic power or special virtue from "flowing away," just as the *snātaka*[38] is, in a similar way, not allowed to sit directly on the bare earth, as well-known "powerful" persons or objects are often supposed to lose their power by having direct contact with the earth.[39]

A King is also forbidden to shave his head for a year after his coronation because it is believed that the hair is filled with virile strength: Rites have put the strength of the water with which he is consecrated into the hair, and for similar reasons, the King may not wash himself.[40] Similarly, the King's divine power wanes if he violates any restrictions placed on him by his position. For example, during the *aśvamedha* the King was required to perform an act of *tapas* (asceticism): by lying every night between his favorite wife's thighs while abstaining

---

37 Ibid. The *aśvamedha* is the horse sacrifice, in which a horse roamed the kingdom for a year.

38 The student after having concluded his study, when he is filled with holy power.

39 Gonda, " Ancient Indian Kingship from the Religious Point of View," 56.

40 Ibid.

from sexual intercourse.[41] Semen retention is a well-known method of achieving *tapas* and is also linked to yogic practices. Similarly, Śiva, though depicted as ithyphallic, never ejaculates. The *Laws of Manu* likewise relate that the King was created from eternal and essential particles of the great *devas*, who in later literature are grouped as "guardians of the world" (*lokapāla*); they are believed to protect the eight main points of the universe.[42] The *lokapāla* surround Mount Meru, the cosmic mountain, at the symbolic center of the world.

This theory also relates to the śāstric notion of the Kali Yuga[43] and the avatar Kalki. Kalki is born in Shambhala at the center of the cosmos, as the Lord of Time; thus, time (personified by the god Kālá, from which Kālī is also derived) exists at the center, for it is regulated by the Sun. The Kali Yuga itself is believed to end when all of the major planets are aligned and not in motion; thus, it ends when time stops, which is represented by Viṣṇu's final avatar. This explains why he is the last incarnation of Viṣṇu, because the decay inherent in the manifold corruption of *ṛta* and *dharma* ceases when it is finally destroyed by the cessation of the passage of time itself. This religious symbolism is not merely deployed at a spiritual and symbolic level; it is connected with the model of the state in India and beyond. As a political system, it is still found within Cambodia's monarchy, where the God-King resides atop Mount Meru, at the center of the world:

41 Ibid., 58-59.

42 Ibid., 60.

43 The Kali Yuga is named after the male demon Kali, who is not to be confused with the Goddess Kālī.

> Yesodharapura, the first city of Angkor, founded towards 900 C.E., formed an enormous square of about two and a half miles on a side, with its sides facing the cardinal points and with the Phnom Bakbang, a small rocky hill, as center. An inscription tells us that this mountain in the center of the capital with the temple on its summit was "equal in beauty to the king of mountains", i.e., to Mount Meru. The temple on Phnom Bakheng contained a Lingam, the phallic symbol of Siva, representing the Devaraja, the "God King," i.e., the divine essence of kingship which embodied itself in the actual king.[44]

Furthermore, a surviving political model based on the divine Solar King still exists in Burma. Burmese chronicles say that Sri Ksetra (Old Prome) on the lower Irrawaddy River, which was the ancient kingdom of the Pyu's capital city, was built by the gods themselves with Indra at their head, and was a replica of Indra's city:

> Sudarsana on the summit of Mount Meru, with thirty-two main gates and a golden palace in its center. The remains of the city show, in fact, a decided attempt at a circular layout though complete regularity has not been achieved. It seems to have been an old custom in Burma that each of the capital's gates corresponded to one of the empire's provinces or vassal states.

---

[44] Robert von Heine-Geldern, " Conceptions of State and Kingship in Southeast Asia" (revised version), in *Far Eastern Quarterly*, Vol. 2 (Michigan: Association for Asian Studies, 1968), 6.

> Thirty-two vassals or heads of provinces with the king as thirty-third in the center would, of course, correspond to the thirty-three gods who reside on the summit of Meru and among whom Indra is king. Thus not only the capital city but the whole empire of the Pyu must have been organized as an image of the heavenly realm of Indra.[45]

Burma's monarchy was structured on this very model, with even the queens' palaces corresponding to the different points of the compass and their chambers forming a circle around the King, whose hall is located at the center of the complex. This emphasizes the role of the King as the center of the universe and as a representative of Indra, the King of the Gods in the paradise on the summit of Mount Meru:[46]

> Hence he is Sun and moon, fire and wind, Yama and Kubera, Varuṇa and Indra. Nobody on earth is able even to gaze at him. Even an infant king is no mortal being, but a great deity (*devatā*) in human form. It is, of course, no matter of indifference that it is these main gods, protectors par excellence, whose essence constitutes his majesty (*pratāpa*). These divinities very significantly represent those functions and activities which are the essential characteristics of kingship. Manu himself already observed that the king like the Sun, burns (*tapati*) eyes and hearts, "nor", he adds,

---

45 Ibid., 7.

46 Ibid.

> "can anybody on earth even gaze on him": the Sun indeed shines, dispels the darkness and its beings; he is the "lord of eyes," all-seeing and the spy (or witness) of the whole world. Like a man of the military class, the Sun slays. The earthly ruler has several qualifications and epithets in common with the great luminary: *pratāpa* is, in the king, his majesty, brilliance or energy, in the Sun, the glowing heat or brilliance; the adjective *pratāpin* means "burning, scorching" as well as "glowing, shining; splendid, powerful, majestic."[47]

Though the King is said to be a combination of these deities, references here allude more to Varuṇa than to other deities, as is demonstrated by the King's title "Lord of Eyes" and his ability to survey the world from a distance, like the earlier description of Varuṇa. The solar features of the King as sovereign are nearly identical to the earlier depiction of Varuṇa. Obviously the *Laws of Manu* draw heavily on the older Vedic conception of the "universal monarch," and these sciences of legislation and polity had a profound impact on the political structure of India and other countries that adopted Hinduism or Buddhism as their religion.

As the embodiment of *dharma* and the representation of divinity on Earth, extreme restrictions were placed upon the king. The list of ethical constraints is much more stringent than they are for modern politicians. As much as the king ruled the people, he was also bound by *dharma* to ensure

47 Gonda, "Ancient Indian Kingship from the Religious Point of View," 60.

their well-being. The king's primary duty was to protect the wealth and happiness of his subjects – the state of the subjects being classed as a reflection of the king's nature. Where the people were prosperous and happy, the king was believed to be divine; where they were miserable or otherwise suffering, the king was thought to have strayed from the path of *dharma* and righteousness. This is amply illustrated in the following statement from Indra to Vasu:

> Accompanied by the gods, he presented himself and told him that a king who prefers asceticism to his duties does not conform to *dharma*, the very foundation of the world; that the *dharma* of the king is to protect the *dharma* of the world, and, consequently, that his eternal salvation was at stake.[48]

On festive occasions intended to promote the general welfare, the King gave satisfaction to the poor and the disabled with gifts of gold. Thus, one of the titles conferred on the King in the *Aitareyabrāhmaṇa* is that of *bhoja*, a term which suggests that one is "liberal or bountiful."[49] Similarly, the word *rājan*, derived from the title *rāja*, is in a significant way often derived from *raj/rajñ* (to make glad, to delight),[50] which clearly explains a sovereign's obligation to the people. Similarly, greedy kings were frowned upon. A king who collected taxes or accepted gifts whilst he neglected his duties to the

48 Georges Dumézil, *The Destiny of a King*, trans. Alf Hiltebeitel (Chicago: University of Chicago Pess, 1988), 61.

49 Gonda, " Ancient Indian Kingship from the Religious Point of View," 48-49.

50 Ibid.

people was regarded as being in violation of his *dharma*, and thus the text states that "[t]he conduct of a monarch who, without guarding his people like a father his son, collects the usual taxes, is most unjust and unbecoming."[51] The *Mahābhārata* also relates this: "[I]f he observes the *dharma* he attains to the dignity of a god; if however, he acts unrighteously, he sinks into hell," calling upon the people to put him to death as if he were a mad dog.[52] The King's duties also extended to meteorological events, and he was believed to be responsible for rainfall. "Indra, seeing that all the *kṣatriya* sovereigns ruled their kingdoms very virtuously, poured down vivifying showers of rain at the proper time and at the proper place, and thus protected all creatures."[53]

The King also has many privileges, however. In his role as a representative of *dharma* and the cosmic order, he also punishes all those who transgress them with impunity, just as Varuṇa did: "As fire is not polluted even though it always burns the creatures of the world (*prajās*), even so, a king is not polluted by inflicting punishment on those who deserve it."[54] The King also has the right and responsibility to maintain order in society by the use of violence; if a war protects the people, then it is a *jus ad bellum*.[55] The King must not wage war by unfair means, however, for Bhishma asks in the *Mahābhārata*: "What kind of ruler would rejoice in an unjust

[51] Ibid., 42-43.

[52] Ibid., 67.

[53] Ibid., 51.

[54] Ibid.

[55] Brekke, "The Ethics of War," 64.

victory (*adharmavijaya*)?"[56] To maintain order and to protect his people, the king has *daṇḍa*, which represents both military power and punishment. In Indian iconography, this is symbolized by the wielding of a rod or scepter:

> The rod is the king and the man, he is the inflicter and he is the chastiser, traditionally regarded as the guarantor for the duty of the four stages of life. The rod alone chastises all subjects, the rod protects them, the rod stays awake while they sleep; wise men know that justice is the rod. Properly wielded, with due consideration, it makes all the subjects happy; but inflicted without due consideration, it destroys everything. Where the rod moves about, black and with red eyes, destroying evil, there the subjects do not get confused, as long as the inflicter sees well.[57]

Just as the King is equivalent to Varuṇa and the Sun, so too does the structure of the microcosm reflect those of the macrocosm; just as the Sun is the center of the solar system around which the planets orbit, the King is placed in a central location of the power structure, a circular construct representing the cosmos and the points of the compass. In ancient Indo-European political theory, power is located at

56 Ibid., 72.

57 Ibid., 61.

the center.[58] This reflects the topology of sacred space, with divine geography being superimposed onto the physical world. It is seen in descriptions where the world consists of a circular central continent, Jambudvipa, surrounded by seven annular oceans and seven annular continents. Zoroastrian texts further divide the world into seven parts, the seven *kišvar*. Still, beneath these, in the very names and distribution of the "sevenths," one perceives a division into five, consisting of the four cardinal points and the center.[59] However, Iranian texts on sovereignty and tradition should be regarded as entirely separate from (and possibly even antithetical to) the Hindu traditions. Ahriman could be an etymological corruption of the name Aryaman, a deity closely linked to Mitra and Varuṇa's sovereignty aspects. As Dumézil points out, such transpositions "may have to do with the Zoroastrian upheaval, which not only demonized patron deities of the warrior class but perhaps extended the halo of rulership to priestly manipulators."[60] Furthermore,

> [...] we know that Indra was one of the main victims of the Zoroastrian reform. He became one of the arch-demons diametrically opposed to the archangels, and his role of warrior,

---

58 In the theories of Celtic kingship, the King is located in the middle, and in Arthurian myth, Arthur is the Sun King, surrounded by a spherical model of twelve Grail knights. Similar motifs are also found in pre-Abrahamic Middle Eastern theories of sovereignty.

59 Dumézil, *The Destiny of a King*, 10.

60 Georges Dumézil, *The Plight of a Sorcerer*, eds. Jaan Puhvel, & David Weeks (Berkeley: University of California Press, 1986), ix.

> rehabilitated, moralized, and placed in the service of the true religion, was divided between the traditional god Mithra, untroublesome for the reformers, and the personified abstraction of victory, Varadragna, in whom the title of the fallen god transparently survived.[61]

Georges Dumézil, by outlining the connection between Vedic and Iranian texts, also makes it clear that he believes the origin of the Āryans (Indo-Europeans) lies in India, and that the line of *kavis* were Indian immigrants to eastern Iran who initiated the Zoroastrian reform.[62] In further support of an "out of India" origin of Iranian sovereignty myths, Dumézil states that the fact that "three of the names of the *kavis* have pre-Zoroastrian forms only leads one to believe that, mythical or historical, they do antedate Zoroaster."[63]

Ultimately, the implication is that the Iranian myths of sovereignty are the results of Vedic deities who were later altered as a result of syncretism and the push towards the monotheistic religions of Judaism and Islam, for the origins of both can be traced back to Zoroastrianism. We can, however, find more relevant applications of sovereignty myths within European traditions, and one example can be found in the Celtic religion:

> Alwyn and Brinley Ress have made an admirable study and which, bringing in the three Indo-European functions complemented by a fourth

61 Ibid., 96-97.

62 Ibid., 91.

63 Ibid., 93.

> term and crowned by a royal power, probably derive from a Druidic doctrine. In the course of the narrative filled with theoretical statements, a man named Fontan is asked by a supernatural being "O Fontan, how has our island been divided, what things were found there [that is, were found in each of its divisions]?" Fontan replies: "Knowledge is in the west, Battle in the North, Prosperity in the East, Music in the South, Royalty in the center."[64]

This is also found in other European traditions, notably Grail myths with King Arthur as the solar sovereign surrounded by knights of the round table, and in Odin, who is seated in the center, with his eye in Mimir's well, demonstrating the same form of omniscience seen in the Vedic god Varuṇa. In India this is also seen in the *lokapālas*, the regional gods of the cardinal points: Varuṇa, the ancient magical sovereign; Indra, the celestial warrior; Kubera, a lord of riches; and Yama, the ruler of the land of the dead.[65] The *Mahābhārata* also relates the legend of Yayāti, who is the mythical first king. Yayati apportions the world between his five sons, who will build the future kingdom of the Pāṇḍavas – representing the four directions with the King at their center. This Vedic model of polity provides a lineage of continuity through the *Mahābhārata* and the well-known text on legislation, the *Laws of Manu*. The latter clearly describes the role and behavior of a king. Moreover, these duties are entwined with those expected of the *kṣatriya varṇa*. The *kṣatriya* were not merely the

64 Dumézil, *The Destiny of a King*, 11.

65 Ibid., 12.

warrior caste; they were also the aristocracy, and as such a higher standard of behavior was required of them. They were a nobility of thought and deed which was expected to protect the Kingdom and uphold the *dharma*. This attitude is expressed via the following excerpts from the *Laws of Manu*:(A king) who knows the sacred law, must inquire into the laws of castes, of districts, of guilds, and of families, and (thus) settle the peculiar law of each.[66]

> I will declare now the duties of kings, (and) show how a king should conduct himself [...] and how (he can obtain) highest success.[67]

> A *kṣatriya* who has received according to the rule the sacrament prescribed by the Veda must duly protect the whole (world).[68]

> A king who, while he protects his people, is deified by (foes), be they equal in strength, or stronger, or weaker, must not shrink from battle, remembering the duty of *kṣatriya*.[69]

> The highest duty of a *kṣatriya* is to protect his subjects, for the king who enjoys the rewards, just mentioned, is bound to (discharge that duty).[70]

---

66 Radhakrishnan & Moore, *A Sourcebook in Indian Philosophy*, 176.

67 Ibid., 186.

68 Ibid.

69 Ibid., 187.

70 Ibid.

The connection between the religious ideal and the relationship between the aristocracy and *dharma* have exerted their influence on models of the state since Vedic times, continuing through the creation of the *Laws of Manu* and reaching their apex of sophistication in the work of the astonishingly brilliant statesman Cāṇakya. His strategies successfully defeated the army of Alexander the Great and founded the first empire in India: the Mauryan Empire, one of the largest and most powerful empires in world history. Aśoka and Chandragupta were the perfect leaders at the helm of a solar-based aristocratic empire. Chandragupta was the first Emperor of India – but without the aid of his chief advisor, Cāṇakya, he never could have successfully united India. Because of this, Cāṇakya is as famous as Chandragupta himself.

IV. CĀNAKYA & THE MAURYAN EMPIRE

CĀNAKYA WAS PERHAPS the most cunning political and military strategist in history. He was so shrewd that even his past is obscured by myth. Some historians even deny his actual existence, claiming that the enigmatic figure known as "Cāṇakya" was perhaps a collective group of authors writing under one name. Given his preference for tactical warfare, it seems likely that Cāṇakya went to great lengths to obscure elements of his life through deliberate subterfuge. He has been called the "Indian Machiavelli" for his stratagems, planned disinformation, and political skulduggery. Cāṇakya nevertheless surpasses everything written by Machiavelli in his quest to install a *Cakravartin* to preside over a new empire. He is more "Machiavellian" than Machiavelli himself was, since his ideas are more complex, incorporating ideas that have no political basis. It is more appropriate to think of him as a hybrid of Machiavelli, Sun Tzu, and religious thought. Although the Mauryan Empire is the most potent embodiment of a civilization built on dharmic principles and caste nobility, Cāṇakya's tactics were merciless in terms of conquest. While he brought a Golden Age to India, he would have undeniably been terrifying as a military and intellectual opponent. Chandragupta's rise to power was thus built on the corpses of his political rivals.

Cāṇakya's tale and that of the Mauryan Empire's success represent one of the fascinating periods in history. It also features another famous figure, Alexander the Great. In 327 BCE, Alexander marched his army into northwest India, traveling through Pakistan and crossing the Indus River in the following year. Though the battle of Hydaspes was a success and King Poros was defeated, this was the beginning of the end for Alexander. His troops – wearied by eight years of incessant fighting, battered by the Indian monsoon's ferocity, and fearful of rumors that opposing kings were then commanding armies equipped with war elephants – refused to cross the Hyphasis (the Beas River, which is east of the city of Lahore in present-day Pakistan). Alexander was then forced to turn back, leaving Greek outposts in the occupied Indian territories.[71] Though the remaining Greek outposts were soon lost, contact between Greece and India remained, and Megasthenes was stationed at the court of Chandragupta Maurya. His accounts are the most important source on this period for Western historians, and it is through these that we know that Alexander's military excursions into India launched

[71] Rashed Uz Zaman, "Kautilya: The Indian Strategic Thinker and Indian Strategic Culture," in *Comparative Strategy*, Vol. 25, No. 3 (Milton Park, Oxfordshire: Routledge, 2007), 233.

Cāṇakya's political career and laid the foundations for the Mauryan Empire, which at its zenith was rivaled only by the Mughal and, later, the British Empire.[72]

Chandragupta Maurya is believed to have begun his military career by fighting against the Greek outposts that Alexander had established along the river Indus. After bringing them under his control, he extended his power eastwards and, in 320 BCE, defeated King Dhana Nanda, seizing the throne of Magadha. Alexander's troops refused to proceed further eastwards after the defeat of King Poros because of rumors about the powerful king who was waiting for them in India's interior. Dhana Nanda had allegedly possessed a powerful army of 200,000 infantrymen, 20,000 horsemen, 2,000 chariots drawn by four horses each, and 3,000 elephants. That Chandragupta could defeat him and occupy his throne when Alexander could not demonstrated how powerful Cāṇakya and Chandragupta's forces were. Under Cāṇakya's guidance, Chandragupta united India as a single power for the first time in history. His grandson was the even more famous Indian Emperor Aśoka, who converted to Buddhism. Through his records we know of the Buddha and the early background of Theravāda Buddhism. Following Aśoka's death, the Mauryan Empire began to decline, and in this weakened state it was eventually crippled by insurgents from the Middle East.

While the lives of Chandragupta and Aśoka are well-documented, very little is known of the *brāhmaṇa* political and military strategist Cāṇakya, whose instructions brought Chandragupta to the

---

72 Ibid.

throne. Cāṇakya was so skilled in political deception and disinformation that his own life has passed into myth. All that is known is that he was born at Chanaka, and his father's name was also Chanaka, so he came to be known as Cāṇakya. Cāṇakya also completed two other important works: the *Cāṇakya Sūtras* (*Rules of Science*) and the *Cāṇakya Rājanītiśātra* (*Science of Government Policies*).[73]

Some scholars doubt whether he even existed, claiming that the *Arthaśāstra* is a literary forgery dating from about the third century CE. Three main pieces of evidence have been used to support this contention:

i. in his *Mahabhashya*, Patanjali mentions Chandragupta and the Mauryas but is silent about Cāṇakya;
ii. even though Megasthenes wrote about the Maurya dynasty, especially about their magnificent capital city and also about Indian society's seven strata, he never mentioned Cāṇakya; and
iii. the *Arthaśāstra* was not written by Cāṇakya but is most likely a compilation of various older texts and ideas. The compilation was probably assembled by scores of individuals rather than one single person.[74]

[73] Balbir S. Sihag, "Kautilya on Moral, Market, and Government Failures," in *International Journal of Hindu Studies*, Vol. 13, No. 1 (New York: Springer, 2009), 86.

[74] Zaman, "Kautilya," 234.

Other authors also point out that many of the concepts used by Cāṇakya are historically associated with the fourth century BCE.[75] Nevertheless, many academics believe Cāṇakya was a real historical personage and not a pseudonym, stating that the fact that there is no mention of Cāṇakya in other records from the period should not be taken as evidence of his non-existence.

As for Megasthenes, some scholars point out that his *Indika* is not available in its entirety; only a few fragments survive in the writings of later Greek historians. It is therefore a wildly unreliable source. However, the various references made in the *Arthaśāstra* to the march of the *Cakravartin* bear a striking resemblance to Alexander's campaign strategy, which is believed to have inspired some of Cāṇakya's military tactics.[76] Given that Cāṇakya had a fondness for espionage, assassinations, and plotting, it is also possible that he deliberately obfuscated parts of his daily life. This is a very feasible strategy for someone who preferred clandestine operations to open warfare. Furthermore, scholars cite sections of Megasthenes' description of Chandragupta's capital and relate it to Cāṇakya's injunction on building fortifications. Megasthenes reported that the city was fortified with palisades. The fortification was shaped like a parallelogram measuring about nine miles in length and about one and a half miles in breadth. It consisted of 570 towers and 64 gates. It has been established that the distances between the towers (or between a tower and the next gate)

[75] Sihag, "Kautilya on Moral, Market, and Government Failures," 92-93.

[76] Zaman, "Kautilya," 235.

as described in Megasthenes' account closely correspond to the distance prescribed for this kind of fortification cited by Cāṇakya in the *Arthaśāstra*.

Despite the few dissenting historians, from the evidence at hand it seems safe to attribute authorship of the *Arthaśāstra* to Cāṇakya, and that any parts which were not penned by him personally could well be textual revisions which were added at a later date.[77] Cāṇakya also features in the *Mudrārākṣasa* (*The Minister's Signet Ring*), a play consisting of seven acts by Viskhadatta which centers on the Nanda dynasty's defeat and Cāṇakya's winning over of the Nanda Chancellor Raksasa to the cause of his royal protégé, Chandragupta.[78]

As such a formidable tactician, Cāṇakya is a rarity in the realm of political theory, and much of his history has been mythologized. Born into a *brāhmaṇa* family, Cāṇakya could never be allowed to rule. It was prophesied that he would reign through another, and by wielding the power of the *kṣatriya*, he established himself as the "puppet master" behind the Empire. Many therefore believe that although Chandragupta reigned as Emperor, Cāṇakya himself was the real ruling power, and it is for this reason that his political texts are studied.

Cāṇakya is rumored to have searched for a suitable child to train for leadership. Once he had found him in Chandragupta, the latter was then trained in the arts of war and politics from childhood, and was finally made Emperor in a manner similar to the way

---

77 Ibid.

78 Ibid., 234.

Merlin prepared Arthur in British myth. Indeed, this was no easy feat, so Cāṇakya was rightfully feared by his opponents as a master strategist, to the extent that he is still called the "Indian Machiavelli" by European scholars. Cāṇakya believed that Alexander's invasion of India was the result of an absence of a centralized, solid Indian empire. The Mauryan Empire, which he was instrumental in founding, was therefore (relatively) centralized and very different from the prevailing republican systems.[79] His most famous work, the *Arthaśāstra*, was not rediscovered until the 1920s and is still studied today both in India and the Occident for military purposes and as a system that could be implemented within the context of modern economics.

---

[79] Kyoung-joon Park, "On the Problem of the Origin of Cakravartin," in *International Journal of Buddhist Thought & Culture*, Vol. 1 (Seoul: International Association for Buddhist Thought & Culture, Academy of Buddhist Studies, 2007), 1.

V. THE CAKRAVARTIN

CĀNAKYA WAS ALSO the first to use the title of "*Cakravartin*," or ruler of the world, and bestowed this on his pupil, Emperor Chandragupta. The word *maṇḍala* also first appears in Cāṇakya's works rather than in religious thought, with which it is more commonly associated, and to which it seems to have been a later addition. Cāṇakya's *maṇḍala* is deployed in a political context, referring to a strategic process in which allegiances were formed and subsequently ended with the aim of empowering Chandragupta. Though the strategy employed in *maṇḍala* theory was efficient and achieved its goal, it was brutal in its implementation. Whoever stood in Cāṇakya's way was eliminated in an expedited fashion. This is not to say his strategies were dishonorable; on the contrary, they were highly noble – for his own citizens. His political rivals, however, all ended up either dead or defeated, by fair means or foul. They were destroyed in wars waged by the *kṣatriya* caste, which composed the bulk of his army. Believing that this caste was best-suited for combat, Cāṇakya and Chandragupta allegedly recruited every *kṣatriya* in the Empire.

Cāṇakya's empire, which was presided over by the *Cakravartin*, has its origins in the *Laws of Manu*. There is an unbroken link of causality showing a direct continuity from Varuṇa's solar rule through the *Laws of Manu* and to the Mauryan Empire's political texts. Cāṇakya begins the *Arthaśāstra* by approaching politics as a science. It is *daṇḍanīti*, or the science of government, but he does not declare it to be the supreme science. *Ānvīkṣikī* (the science of logic), the three Vedas, *vārtā* (agriculture, cattle-breeding, and trade), and *daṇḍanīti* are referred to as the four sciences.[80] Of these, Cāṇakya believes the *ānvīkṣikī* (philosophy) to be the most important, despite his own involvement in politics:

> When seen in the light of these sciences, the science of *Ānvīkṣikī* is most beneficial to the world, keeps the mind steady and firm in weal and woe alike, and bestows excellence of foresight, speech, and action. Light to all kinds of knowledge, easy means to accomplish all kinds of acts and receptacle of all kinds of virtues, is the science of *Ānvīkṣikī* ever held to be.[81]

Cāṇakya here treats the science of logic as the initial premise from which those skills which underlie all other sciences arise, as a "foundation" to be built upon by further study and knowledge. In this manner, Cāṇakya reveals his essentially brāhmaṇic nature, despite being at the helm of a

80 Radhakrishnan & Moore, *A Sourcebook in Indian Philosophy*, 197.

81 Ibid., 198.

vast military empire conquered and governed by *kṣatriyas*. Though Cāṇakya is often perceived as an unscrupulous political tactician, this is not entirely the case. Only the Mauryan Empire's political rivals were targeted for assassination. Regarding the governance of the people and the Empire, Cāṇakya is exceptionally benevolent. A strong current of spirituality is present, which ties his work directly to its predecessor, the *Laws of Manu*. This provides a consistent legacy between his political theory and the Vedic past. When speaking of the Vedas, Cāṇakya says:

> For the world, when maintained in accordance with the Vedas, will ever prosper and not perish. Therefore, the king shall never allow the people to swerve from their *dharma* [...] For, when *adharma* overwhelms *dharma*, the king himself will be destroyed. [...] [The observance of] one's own *dharma* leads to heaven and eternal bliss. When *dharma* is transgressed, the resulting chaos leads to the extermination of this world.[82]

While Cāṇakya's military and political strategies were revolutionary, his spiritual ideas were profoundly traditional and conservative. They promote the ruler as the embodiment of *dharma*. The King, for Cāṇakya, should be a beneficent paragon of virtue to his people. He is therefore required to maintain a high standard of behavior above and beyond that of the common people. According to Cāṇakya's

---

[82] Sihag, "Kautilya on Moral, Market, and Government Failures," 95.

treatise, the King is instructed in how to become the *Cakravartin*, the supreme solar sovereign who acts as one modeled on the ancient ideal of Varuṇa and guided by the *Laws of Manu* to become the perfect leader. Under Cāṇakya's guidance, Chandragupta was not merely a figurehead for political propaganda; he was trained in morality, *dharma*, and wisdom to act as the *Cakravartin*. Chandragupta followed the texts to become the perfect spiritual leader. After his reign, he took up residence with the Jains. His son Aśoka assumed a similar behavior model. Despite amassing a vast army, he did not engage in any unjust acts. Instead, he devoted himself to the newly-emerged Buddhist tradition and spent money on public works to keep the people happy.

Kaultiya's political teaching also had an impact on the development of Buddhism, with the integration of the *maṇḍala*, which had first been used in his political and military strategies, into its esoteric symbolism. He likewise asserted that the *Cakravartin* is the terrestrial alternative to a Bodhisattva, or a future Buddha, and this knowledge spread through Southeast Asia and India. Oung Zaya, who reigned from 1752 to 1760, was the founder of Burma's last dynasty, and took the name Alaungpaya, which designated him as an Embryo Buddha. His son, King Bodawpaya (1782-1819), claimed outright to be the Bodhisattva Maitreya, with a similar mantle being later assumed by King Taksin of Siam (1767-1782).[83]

It is written in the *Arthaśāstra* that Cāṇakya saw a direct link between the people and the leader,

---

[83] Heine-Geldern, "Conceptions of State and Kingship in Southeast Asia," *Far Eastern Quarterly*, Vol. 2 , 12.

saying that "[t]he happiness of the subjects is the happiness of the king; their welfare, his; his own pleasure is not his good, but the pleasure of his subjects is his good."[84] The King, must therefore serve the people and abide by his *dharma* as laid out in the Śāstras (scriptures). Although the nature of kingship is sacred, the individual who holds the position is not.[85] For Cāṇakya, the monarchy is a human institution, and the role of the King is held by a mortal human being; the King is expected to be more than a mere human being, however, since he is the protector of *dharma*.[86] Though he was not possessed of superhuman powers, his conduct was expected to be nothing less than divine. In this regard, Cāṇakya espouses several strict rules for kings to follow if they wish to be successful and enrich their kingdoms by serving as models of good conduct.

In the *Arthaśāstra*'s subsequent sections, it is evident that while the *Cakravartin* holds political power, he serves the people and does not expect the people to serve him, as the guidelines imposed by Cāṇakya are incredibly rigid. The fact that discipline and self-governance is one of the principal edicts Cāṇakya associates with the King's dharmic function is made clear in his explanations of how the King's personality is entwined with the people and the welfare of the kingdom:

---

84 Radhakrishnan & Moore, *A Sourcebook in Indian Philosophy*, 193.

85 Aseem Prakash, "*State and Statecraft in Kautilya's Arthasastra*: A Paper Presented at the Fall Semester Mini-Conference Organized by the Workshop in Political Theory and Policy Analysis" (Indiana University, 1998), 11.

86 Ibid.

> If a king is energetic, his subjects will be equally energetic. If he is reckless, they will not only be reckless likewise but also eat into his works. Besides, a reckless king will easily fall into the hands of his enemies. Hence the king shall ever be wakeful.
>
> [...]
>
> Of a king, the religious vow is his readiness to action; satisfactory discharge of duties is his performance of sacrifice; equal attention to all is the offer of fees and ablution towards consecration.
>
> [...]
>
> In the happiness of his subjects lies his happiness; in their welfare his welfare; whatever pleases himself he shall not consider as good, but whatever pleases his subjects he shall consider as good. Hence the king shall ever be active and discharge his duties; the root of wealth is activity and of evil its reverse.
>
> In the absence of activity acquisitions present and to come will perish; by activity, he can achieve both his desired ends and abundance of wealth.[87]

The role of upholding *dharma* and justice is also evident:

---

[87] Radhakrishnan & Moore, *A Sourcebook in Indian Philosophy*, 201-202.

> *Dharma* is eternal truth holding its sway over the world; *vyavahāra*, evidence, is in witness; *cāritra*, history, is to be found in the tradition of the people; and the order of kings is what is called *śāsana*.
>
> [...]
>
> As the duty of the king consists in protecting his subjects with justice, its observance leads him to heaven. He who does not protect his people or upsets the social order wields his royal power in vain.
>
> [...]
>
> The king who administers justice in accordance with sacred law, evidence, history, and edicts of kings, which is the fourth, will be able to conquer the whole world bounded by the four quarters.[88]

The King is also prescribed a stringent daily routine with hours allotted to different stately tasks, and very little of that time is recreational. His day and night are divided into eight *nālikās* (each one-and-a-half hours), with specific tasks for each *nālikā*.[89] There can be no doubt that the real mastermind behind the rise of the Mauryan Empire was not the *Cakravartin*, but Cāṇakya, who plotted and planned every contingency and military task down to the finest detail. Together they quite possibly formed the

---

88 Ibid., 203.

89 Park, "On the Problem of the Origin of Cakravartin," 11.

best historical representative of Georges Dumézil's theory of dual sovereignty, where the *brāhmaṇa* and *kṣatriya* were not opposed but rather combined forces, welding both intellectual genius and the might of the militia together into a single power in the service of the Kingdom.

Cāṇakya also relates the ideal characteristics inherent in the leader's personality, providing guidelines for the selection of further kings. It is clear that he did not believe the position was necessarily hereditary, but should rather be relegated to that individual who embodied all the desired traits. To be a good King, Cāṇakya believed that one must have the necessary predisposition to uphold *dharma* and become a sovereign who is an asset to the people. Cāṇakya describes the desirable qualities of a King as follows:

> Possessed of a sharp intellect, strong memory, and keen mind, energetic, powerful, trained in all kinds of arts, free from vice, capable of paying in the same coin by way of awarding punishments or rewards, possessed of dignity, capable of taking remedial measures against dangers, possessed of foresight, ready to avail himself of opportunities when afforded in respect of place, time, and manly efforts, clever enough to discern the causes necessitating the cessation of treaty or war with an enemy, or to lie in wait keeping treaties, obligations and pledges, or to avail himself of his enemy's weak points, making jokes with no loss of dignity or secrecy, never brow-beating and casting haughty and stern looks, free from

> passion, anger, greed, obstinacy, fickleness, haste and back-biting habits, talking to others with a smiling face, and observing customs as taught by aged persons - such is the nature of self-possession.[90]

What Cāṇakya is describing as his ideal model of sovereignty is not so much an individual who only has academic training in politics but who also possesses a natural temperament suited to leadership. This is significant because Cāṇakya dwells on the moral integrity and character required for a good leader. Thus, the essential requirements are inborn, and are primarily related to the cognitive faculties of intelligence and wisdom. Though a mortal, Cāṇakya's model for the *Cakravartin* therefore bears the mark of the sacred, and this will enable him to rise to power as a protector of *dharma*. This role is the King's primary function, just as it was Varuṇa's. Though mortal, the King's behavior must be that of a god on Earth. This is fully in accord with traditional Hindu thought: "They say that the king is a human being; but I consider you to be a god, whose behavior, if it is in accordance with *dharma* (norms) and *artha* (political utility) is superhuman."[91]

Cāṇakya definitely expected superhuman qualities from "human" kings: Chandragupta, Bindusar, and Aśoka matched his ideal, but their successors did not. It is also quite clear that he believed certain types of people are unsuitable to

---

90 Radhakrishnan & Moore, *A Sourcebook in Indian Philosophy*, 205-206.

91 Gonda, "Ancient Indian Kingship from the Religious Point of View," 36.

be in positions of power, and the poor leadership of such individuals will ultimately destroy any kingdom over which they reign. In a true traditional state, certain types of people should thus be automatically excluded from entering into positions of authority based on their lack of personal qualities; the right to rule must only be bestowed on those whose first duty is to their kingdom and serving the people. As a prerequisite for access to power, the King must be taught the meaning of *dharma* and *artha*, and must be capable of great self-restraint:

> Therefore, a prince should be taught what is *dharma* and *artha*, not what is unrighteous and materially harmful [...] The sole aim of all branches of knowledge is to inculcate restraint over senses... A king who has no self-control and gives himself up to excessive indulgence in pleasures will soon perish, even if he is the ruler of all four corners of the earth.[92]

Such references occur more than once, and the King's need for good personal conduct and the ability to uphold *dharma* are repeatedly emphasized:

> A *rajarishi* (a king, wise like a sage) is one who: has self-control, having conquered the (inimical temptations) of the senses, cultivates the intellect by association with elders...is ever active in promoting the security and welfare of the people...endears himself to his people by enriching them and doing good to them [and] avoid[s] daydreaming, capriciousness,

92 Sihag, "Kautilya on Moral, Market, and Government Failures," 96.

> falsehood and extravagance [...] A *rajarishi* shall always respect those councillors and *purohitas* who warn him of the dangers of transgressing the limits of good conduct, reminding him sharply (as with a goad) of the times prescribed for various duties and caution him even when he errs in private [...] (Government by) Rule of Law, which alone can guarantee security of life and welfare of the people, is, in turn, dependent on (the) self-discipline (of the king). [...] In the happiness of his subjects lies his happiness; in their welfare his welfare. He shall not consider as good only that which pleases him but treat as beneficial to him whatever pleases his subjects.[93]

All else was considered by Cāṇakya to be political incompetence and folly of the highest order. The King was expected to obey his *rayja dharma* and by doing so he was to display *ātmā vrata* (self-control) and abandon the "six enemies – *kama* (lust), *krodha* (anger), *lobha* (greed), *mana* (vanity), *mada* (haughtiness), and *harsha* (overjoy)."[94]

The *Arthaśāstra* primarily offers the reader two teachings: how to acquire a kingdom via warfare and how to maintain it. During the era in which the *Arthaśāstra* was composed, India was in a state of bloody internal conflicts between small kingdoms. It was a time of perpetual infighting while the armies of Alexander were advancing from the north. Cāṇakya did not create the *Arthaśāstra* out of megalomania or the need for conflict; it was rather composed with the concept of what the Romans called *jus ad*

---

93 Ibid.

94 Park, "On the Problem of the Origin of Cakravartin," 11.

bellum (the conditions for the use of armed force) in mind. India was crippled by war, and needed a single ruler to bring peace and unify the country as an empire strong enough to deter foreign invasions. War was therefore legitimized to protect the people, and it was in fact essential in the name of the greater good; it was justified, and therefore in accordance with *dharma*. Despite the fact that they were at the head of a powerful empire, neither Cāṇakya nor Chandragupta were warmongers. Once India was unified, they did not seek to invade their neighboring countries despite certainly possessing an army which could have quickly conquered them. Cāṇakya realized that further conquest was a destructive strategy in the long run, and thus against *dharma*. Although his armies had destroyed the weaker kings of India and abolished their reigns, it was consistent with the concept of *jus ad bellum* (justified war) because such wars were waged to protect the people.

It is also notable that Cāṇakya was firmly against causing civilian casualties. Despite frequently ordering assassinations of political rivals, he advised his armies not to harm women, civilians, cows (as they are considered sacred), or damage farmlands. In fact, Cāṇakya was extraordinarily humanitarian for his era, and although slavery was common, he even passed laws protecting slaves by forbidding his soldiers to copulate with or mistreat them. According to Cāṇakya, the state (King) had three primary responsibilities: seeing to the protection, nurturing and administration, and welfare of its citizens.

Cāṇakya further recommended that a government should help the less fortunate members of society. He likewise advocated providing insurance against natural disasters to everyone,[95] and even put privacy laws into effect, preventing civilians from being spied upon. It is therefore impossible to classify Cāṇakya in terms of the contemporary political spectrum, for although his empire was conservative, martial, and based on traditional Vedic teachings, he also established models for social welfare programs that would not be seen again in politics for centuries.

Finally, the *Arthaśāstra* also records progress that was made in the sciences during Cāṇakya's time, describing the processing of gems, minerals, metallic ores, metals, and alloys, and displaying the author's aptitude for developing a scientific methodology.

It is reasonable to assume that Cāṇakya was not merely crafting propaganda; he really did take *dharma* very seriously and was attempting to establish humanitarian principles in his model of the State. Much of his political theory is directly derived from the spiritual teachings of the Vedas, particularly the "doctrine of *Trivarga*" (three goals), in which "[e]very man was required to strive to satisfy his spiritual needs by fulfilling his religious and moral duties *(dharma);* his material needs by acquiring the necessities of life, property, wealth and power *(artha);* his instinctive desires by following the dictates of love (*kama*)."[96] These three principles were later extended in Indian thought by the addition of a fourth: *mokṣa* (deliverance from the cycle of death and rebirth). This was a development based on the *Law of Manu*, where it states:

---

95 Sihag, B. S.,"Kautilya on Moral, Market, and Government Failures," pp. 84-85.

96 Prakash, "State and Statecraft in Kautilya's *Arthasastra*," 4.

> (some declare that) the chief good consists in (the acquisition of) spiritual merit and wealth, (others place it) in (the gratification of) desire and (the acquisition of) wealth, (others) in (the acquisition of) spiritual merit alone, and (others say that the acquisition of) wealth alone is the chief good here (below), but the (correct) decision is that it is the aggregate of (these) three.

This illustrates the extent to which Cāṇakya was influenced by Vedic ideas.

VI. THE ARTHAŚĀSTRA

CĀNAKYA LIVED IN a transitory period which saw the old Vedic ways beginning to diminish and new traditions emerging, such as that of the Jains (and to which Chandragupta would convert), which was followed by Buddhism. Cāṇakya's political philosophy remained predominantly Vedic, however, and he believed that a nation would grow at a faster rate if its people were anchored to Vedic values, since he thought that Vedic values promoted economic prosperity, which in turn helped in the preservation of these core values.[97] Cāṇakya's ideas therefore served to revitalize and empower the older Vedic tradition at a time when India was undergoing a significant period of change. This is exemplified in the opening of the *Arthaśāstra*:

> This *Śāstra* has been made by him who from intolerance quickly rescued the scriptures and

[97] Sihag, "Kautilya on Moral, Market, and Government Failures," 84.

> the science of weapons and the earth which had passed to the Nanda king.[98]

This is Cāṇakya's core tenet given that he, who sees himself as the savior of both the Vedic tradition and an empire, declares himself to have preserved both the sacred scriptures and the army from what he believes to have been an ineffectual and corrupt political regime that was predestined for defeat at his and Chandragupta's hands.

The *Arthaśāstra* is also unique in the regard that it is unabashedly a manual for achieving political power composed, not by a theorist or scholar, but rather by a man who actually succeeded in establishing an empire. From this one can assume that its strategy is brutally efficient when fully enacted. The *Arthaśāstra* is not only a treatise on politics, sacred kingship, and economics, but is also a military text prescribed for conquest. Cāṇakya, therefore, directs his writing towards the "king desirous of fresh conquests," in order to create a *Cakravartin*.[99]

In terms of strategic positioning in war, Cāṇakya identifies three forms: *prakashayudda* (open war, battle in the normal sense); *kutayudda* (treacherous war, a war where the enemy is attacked in a variety of ways), and *tusniyudda* (secret war, which involves attacking the enemy using secret agents and occult devices).[100] Through these three forms, Cāṇakya enacts a Six-Fold Policy that is

---

98 Radhakrishnan & Moore, *A Sourcebook in Indian Philosophy*, 221.

99 Zaman, "Kautilya," 236.

100 Ibid., 238.

designed to obliterate opponents and incorporate their kingdoms into his own: this policy for dealing with political rivals is then broken down into further instruments, or *upāyas*. Of these scholars disagree on actual numbers with George Modelski referring to four instruments: *sama* (conciliation), *dāna* (gift), *bheda* (dissension), and *daṇḍa* (punishment); to this Heinrich Zimmer adds three additional ones: *māyā* (deceit), *upekṣā* (indifference), and *indrajāla*. Imtiaz Ahmed, however, lists five instruments as methods for conquest:

> *i.* *Sama* (conciliation): The ruler must attempt conciliation when success in a dangerous situation is unlikely.
>
> *ii.* *Dāna* (gift): The policy of *dāna* is to be applied to inferior kings and discontented people with the avowed purpose of winning them over without bloodshed.
>
> *iii.* *Bheda* (dissension): If *dāna* fails to do its work then the policy of "sowing the seeds of dissension" is to be followed. Its primary purpose is to create chaos and confusion amongst enemies and neutralize their threat.
>
> *iv.* *Māyā-Indrajāla* (deceit and pretense): The ruler could undertake certain tactical maneuvers to outsmart the enemy. These could range from the use of nonaggression pacts or treaties to lull the enemy into a false sense of security, to the policies of wearing a mask of moral probity, religious righteousness or citing moral righteousness to mask one's intentions and attain them through deceit and pretense.

> v. *Daṇḍa* (open attack or war): If all the above instruments fail to contain the enemy then the policy of coercion or open attack is to be undertaken. Since war is a serious matter, however, it is not to be undertaken in haste but is to be pursued only after careful consideration of the enemy's financial condition and the level of popular support which the enemy enjoys.[101]

Cāṇakya also refined the roles of the *brāhmaṇa* and the *kṣatriya* concerning their social function: "It is declared in the Vedas that the goal which is reached by sacrificers, after performing the final ablutions, in sacrifices in which the priests have been duly paid for, is the very goal which brave men are destined to attain."[102] Thus he makes it clear that for the *kṣatriya varṇa* war is the equivalent of the *brāhmaṇic* sacrifice. He clearly elucidates that the duty of a *kṣatriya* is study, the performance of sacrifice, giving gifts, military occupation, and the protection of life. As such, the importance of war occupies a central position in the *Arthaśāstra.* Once victory is achieved, the King also enacts their legislative function and wield the violence of the state against criminal and seditious elements within the King's own territory.[103] Cāṇakya interpreted failure to protect the Kingdom from subversive elements as the sign of a weak and decadent King who "fails to protect the people from thieves and robs them himself"; the perceived presence of crime in society was the result of his

---

101 Ibid.

102 Brekke, " The Ethics of War," 78-79.

103 Ibid., 80-82.

poor governance by the King.[104] The condition of *arājakatā* (anarchy) was viewed with distaste as it militated against the practicing of *dharma*; many ancient Vedic texts refer to *mātsyanyāya* (Law of the Fish), which prevails in the state of nature. Laws themselves were derived from four sources: *dharma* (sacred law), *vyavahāra* (evidence), *dāna* (history and custom), and *rājaśāsana* (edicts of the king).[105] In the case of conflict between the various laws, *dharma* was supreme. *Rājaśāsana* ordered the relationship between the three major social groupings – the citizen, the association, and the state – while the constitutional rules at the state level were specified in the *rājaśāsana,* but the constitutional rules at the level of the association were to be decided by the members of the association.[106] In the cases of extremely bad kings, Cāṇakya also attributes to them a criminal function in not serving the people – "A decadent king [...] oppresses the people by demanding gifts, seizing what he wants and grabbing for himself and his favorites the produce of the country," and "fails to give what ought to be given and exacts what he cannot rightly take," and who "by his indolence and negligence destroys the welfare of his people:"[107] In the interests of the Kingdom's prosperity, a King should also be diligent in foreseeing the possibility of calamities, trying to avert them before they arise, overcoming those which do happen, removing all subsequent obstructions to economic activity

104 Kautilya on Moral, Market, and Government Failures," 92-93

105 Prakash, "State and Statecraft in Kautilya's Arthasastra," 13.

106 Ibid.

107 Park, "On the Problem of the Origin of Cakravartin," 8-10.

and preventing loss of revenue to the state.[108] The *Arthaśāstra* conceptualizes the state itself as having seven elements:[109]

1. *Svāmī* (Monarch)
2. *Amātya* (Officials)
3. *Jānapada* (Population and Territory)
4. *Durga* (Fort)
5. *Koṣa* (Treasury)
6. *Bala* (Military)
7. *Surhit* (Ally)[110]

The King himself derived his power from three sources – *prabhushakti* (the power of the army and the treasury), *mantashakti* (advice of wise men, specifically the Council of Ministers), and *utsahshakti* (charisma).[111] In addition to the Council of Ministers, there was also an inner cabinet — consisting of the chief minister, the chief priest, the military commander, and the Crown Prince — and the outer cabinet. To ensure that they did not overstep their respective limits, the Superintendent of Accounts had to codify every association's history, customs, and traditions. Except in the case of *Raj Purohita*, the scribe (*brāhmaṇa*), and the army (*kṣatriya*), there were no *varṇa* restrictions for the posts of high-level officials. Thus, upward mobility in the hierarchy was based on merit, suitability,

---

108 Sihag, "Kautilya on Moral, Market, and Government Failures," 83.

109 Park, " On the Problem of the Origin of Cakravartin," 8-10.

110 Ibid.

111 Prakash, "State and Statecraft in Kautilya's Arthasastra," 10.

and fulfilling other qualifications laid down for these posts. Despite being Vedic, Cāṇakya's political system had no rigid power structure and was instead flexible and meritocratic.

There are also occurrences in Cāṇakya's writings which describe ideas no longer present in the modern era. For example, though he made use of political spies, there were privacy laws that prevented spying on civilians, provided insurance against disasters, and imposed sanctions on greedy merchants who exploited the people – something which has gone out of vogue in modernity, where consumers are inundated with debt and misuse of financial power. In this light, Cāṇakya can be seen as mistrusting traders, believing them to be thieves, with a propensity for forming cartels in order to fix prices, generating excessive profits, and dealing in stolen property. Heavy fines were prescribed for discouraging such offenses by traders, with a view toward consumer protection. On a similar note, he also had laws to deal with petty bureaucrats, who were apparently a problem even in his day and age. Being aware of the difficulty of detecting corruption at the bureaucratic level, Cāṇakya stated:

> Just as it is impossible to know when a fish moving in water is drinking it, so it is impossible to find out when government servants in charge of undertakings misappropriate money [...] It is possible to know even the path of birds flying in the sky but not the ways of government servants who hide their (dishonest) income.[112]

112 Sihag, "Kautilya on Moral, Market, and Government Failures," 92-93.

A technique he deployed to keep a check on the bureaucracy was decentralized-polycentric political arrangements which resulted in empowering the local guilds. Thus the bureaucrats had to reckon with an effective local power center that was aware of the royal edicts which prevented them from embezzling funds. Cāṇakya also identifies thirteen types of undesirable persons who amass wealth secretly by causing injury to the population (corrupt judges and magistrates; heads of villages or departments who extort money from the public; perjurers and procurers of perjury; those who practice witchcraft, black magic or sorcery; poisoners; narcotic dealers; and counterfeiters and adulterators of precious metals) – when secret agents exposed them, they were either to be exiled or made to pay adequate compensation proportionate to the gravity of the offense.[113]

113 Ibid.

VII. CONCLUSION

THE GOLDEN AGE of the Mauryan Empire established by Cāṇakya's treatise eventually deteriorated as kings no longer followed its advice and distanced themselves from the model of the "dharmic king"; this, coupled with regression from the wisdom of the Vedas, resulted in a political decline that was disastrous for India. Chandragupta and Cāṇakya's solar empire, which had successfully united India and defeated Alexander the Great began to collapse and finally met its end at the hands of a Muslim invasion in the 8th century. Without the solid military organization advocated by Cāṇakya, India was reduced to a shadow of her former glory and became an easy target for foreign aggressors. However, Cāṇakya's political influence nevertheless continued for more than 2,000 years after his death – surviving in esoteric Buddhist and Jain texts and in political systems. The *maṇḍala* itself, which was first citied in his theory, still exists in Buddhism. More importantly, unlike other political theorists from ancient times, Cāṇakya is making a spectacular reappearance in economic theory. His ideas have been studied as an alternative to the modern financial system, which many view as an increasingly impotent model destined to collapse. To this day, he is likewise studied as a strategist by the military and defense theorists. Offering a cohesive unity of spirituality, wealth, power, and welfare for the people, Cāṇakya's model is nowhere near as dated as it may at first appear – much of it, in fact, is extremely relevant to the field of political science today. Cāṇakya offers a real alternative that has already been proven to be highly successful.

Furthermore, the model still exists among the monarchies of South Asia, where the cosmic and divine role of the King was and still is especially emphasized in the coronation ritual. One of its principal features consists in the King sitting on a throne representing Mount Meru and being surrounded by eight *brāhmaṇas* as representatives of the eight *Lokapālas,* the guardian gods of the eight directions, and four maids of honor, representing the four cardinal points. They in turn render homage to the king. [114] Just as in *maṇḍala* theory and the old Vedic imagery of Varuṇa, the monarch is represented by the Sun at the spiritual and cosmic center. An official document published on the occasion of the coronation of King Sisowath of Cambodia in 1906 also identifies the King with Mount Meru itself, his right eye representing the Sun, his left eye the moon, his arms and legs the four cardinal points, the six-tiered umbrella above his head the six lower heavens, his pointed crown the spire of Indra's palace on

[114] Heine-Geldern, "Conceptions of State and Kingship in Southeast Asia," 9.

Meru's summit and his slippers the Earth.[115] Despite the differing imagery, the King is again placed at the spiritual center, occupying a sacred central point.

Beginning with the figure of Varuṇa, the solar monarch who sees all, invested with the power to preserve *dharma* and punish those who dare to violate *ṛta*, his cosmic order, the idea of the Sun as a model for the King and of political power has never died; indeed, it is a universal archetype which can never die, as it is present in all traditional power structures. Ruling first on his own, and then coupled with Mitra, the influence of the Vedic gods perished as newer ones rose to power in India – thus, the law codes were changed to become the *Laws of Manu*. When this, in turn, started to lose influence, Cāṇakya, taking it upon himself to rescue both the sacred science of the Vedas and the art of war, planned what is perhaps the single most extraordinary political operation in history, raising a single boy and training him to conquer a continent while amassing an army of *kṣatriya* in the process. The fact that one person composed a text such as the *Arthaśāstra* to commandeer an empire essentially suggests that Cāṇakya planned and plotted to rise to power long before he began to enact it's tenets in practice.

The *Arthaśāstra* is unique. It is an ancient text that is peculiarly advanced and humanitarian for its era. Citizens are protected from corrupt financial institutions, civilians are unharmed in war, petty bureaucrats are controlled and kept out of power, insurance is offered for disasters, and welfare is provided for the people. Moreover, it

115 Ibid., 10.

repeatedly emphasizes the need for *dharma* and the transcendent characteristics of the leader, who essentially serves the people.

Following the end of Chandragupta's reign, his grandson, Aśoka, would then go on to become the greatest ruler in Indian history as well as a national hero.

Actions speak a thousand words. The Vedic system of polity produced great heroic leaders and built an empire. So why study the *Arthaśāstra*? For one crucial reason: Cāṇakya's science of politics worked.

www.ingramcontent.com/pod-product-compliance
Lightning Source LLC
Chambersburg PA
CBHW051802040426
42446CB00007B/472
* 9 7 8 0 6 4 5 6 7 0 0 0 4 *